The Church Children's Home in a Changing World

By

Alan Keith-Lucas

Chapel Hill

THE UNIVERSITY OF NORTH CAROLINA PRESS

PRINTED BY THE SEEMAN PRINTERY, DURHAM, N. C.

Foreword

THIS BOOK PULLS together fourteen articles and papers given in the past six or seven years to regional or denominational groups interested in the care of children away from home. Most of these papers have been either mimeographed or published but have had limited circulation. It is my hope that they will be of use not only to institutional personnel but to board members and to others interested in the remarkable and exciting changes that have occurred in Children's Homes during the past ten or fifteen years.

As will be obvious from these papers, I have great faith in the church-sponsored Children's Home and indeed look to it to provide leadership in the field of child care for many years to come. In a very real sense these articles are not my creation; they stem from the thinking and the experiments of the Homes themselves. I wish I could acknowledge their individual contribution, but this would entail listing more than a hundred and fifty homes with which I have been associated through the Group Child Care Project, the Chapel Hill Workshops, the Division of Homes and Christian Welfare of the Presbyterian Church (U.S.) and a number of other organizations from Florida to Texas.

Inevitably in such a collection there will be some repetition of ideas. The truth, as any one man may see it, does not change between an address to a Baptist Group in January and a regional conference in May. Where repetition is too obvious I have tried to eliminate it. Otherwise I have left these papers as they were given, except for topical references.

My particular thanks are due to the *Christian Scholar, Charity and Children, Connie Maxwell, News-n-Views,* and *Public Welfare News* (the last two published by the North Carolina State Board of Public Welfare in Raleigh, N.C.), for permission to reproduce material previously published by them.

Contents

The Church Children's Home
in a Changing World

1.

The Church Children's Home in a Changing World*

PROBABLY NO ACTIVITY in social service or in the church has developed and changed so radically in the last twenty years as that of the church home for children. Those who are in the work know it. A few struggle somewhat vainly against it, trying to persuade themselves that things have not changed or that change can be delayed, but the majority have accepted the challenge and are constantly asking themselves what new conditions demand of them. They may at times—and who does not?—wish that they were back in the good old days when running a church institution was a fairly simple job, when most of the children they had were orphans who came to them in infancy and stayed until they were grown, when the institution was a little unit of its own apart from the rest of the community, when all that they had to worry about was raising money, food, clothing, buildings, and the best way of maintaining Christian training and discipline in their little flocks. Not that these were easy tasks. They demanded courage and skill and devotion. But in the main they were clear-cut, uncomplicated tasks whose purposes were easy to grasp. But these days are gone forever. If the church tries to recall them it can only do so at the cost of living under an illusion, of forfeiting its rightful leadership in the life of the nation, of being not conservative (which churches have the right to be) but reactionary and obscurantist and, even worse, derelict in its responsibility to meet human need.

That churches are meeting this challenge is one of the most encouraging things in the present picture. But more important even than rising to a challenge is the way in which one does so. The outstanding characteristic of the institutional executive in the church today, and what makes working with him the deeply satisfying thing that it is, is his humility where by human standards he has no reason to be humble. It is his spirit of enquiry, his willingness to learn, his consciousness that he does not and cannot have all the answers, which

* Given to the First Annual Child Care Institute, Baptist General Convention of Texas, Highland Lakes Baptist Encampment, June 1958.

is his greatest strength. In this he differs only too often from some secular social workers and social scientists. Moreover, he is making neither of the two mistakes into which it is all too easy for the church institution to fall.

These are, on the one hand, to be suspicious of technical and professional knowledge on the grounds that it is secular, hoping somehow that the piety of the church will by itself provide answers to even the most complicated of questions, ignoring advances in such sciences as psychiatry or such disciplines as social work, insisting that church work is "different" and thus can be left to operate in a backwater of ignorance; on the other, to become so much engrossed with sociological or psychological "facts" and theories that the church-sponsored child-care program becomes merely an up-to-date but essentially secular child-care program run by a church, without its purposes, its means, and its insights being illuminated by its essential Christian nature. And at the very core of this nature is not only love and forgiveness, which other religions also treasure but that greatest of all and perhaps the only specifically Christian virtue—humility, the consciousness of the very limitations of our imperfect human nature, of our fallibility, of the unbridgeable gap between God's will and what we by our own efforts can do.

Thus, in attempting to speak to you on the church institution, I am forever conscious that all I can contribute is a sort of summing up of what has been tried, or, it would seem, ought to be tried, or what looks likely, without any claim at all to have arrived at a "truth." I am also conscious of the wisdom of many men with whom I respectfully disagree, and, particularly, of the fact that every church, every institution, has a wisdom of its own—one that arises from its experience, from the particular problems it has to meet, from the children whom it serves and the people who serve it. You may therefore find in what we discuss here suggestions or ideas which you may genuinely feel do not apply to the institution in whose running you have a hand, or do not do so at this time. Where this arises from genuine difference, disagreement on your part can only be salutary. Where, of course, it arises from an unreal difference, an illusion or area of blindness about the real nature of the church's problems or work, I hope that this may become plain to you. And where the illusion or blindness is mine, I hope that you will try in Christian charity to convince me.

The changes which have taken place in the last twenty or thirty years, which present so great a challenge to the church institution for children, seem to me to be four in number. One is a change in the composition of society itself, one a change in its organization, one the result of new technical knowledge and one a matter of changed thinking within the church itself. By providence or coincidence these four have tended to reinforce each other, so that by and large the change is all in the same direction.

The first great change has been in the needs of children whom the church is called to serve. Part of this change has a medical base. The average span of life has been greatly increased. Far fewer people die today while their children are young. There are therefore far fewer orphans than there used to be. But this does not mean that there are fewer children needing care. As a matter of fact, there are more. Many more families today are faced with problems of long-time illness, and this is particularly true of the mental diseases and of that shadowy land that lies between inadequacy or unacceptable behavior or neglect, on the one hand, and medically diagnosed neurosis or psychosis, on the other—the whole very difficult problem of the person who is part sinner and part sick, but who nevertheless cannot care for his children well.

To this the growing complexity of modern life, the anxieties of a post-war world, and the "unsettled times" in which traditional values seem to have lost their power to comfort millions of men, have played their part. We can and do deplore it but we have to admit that it is true. Thus, although the child today is as effectually "homeless" as he used to be, he is homeless in a different way—homeless and yet, in many cases, with both of his parents alive. This makes it harder for the child to accept comfortably his own need to be in an institution. While, objectively, he may see that it is impossible for him to live at home, he is constantly hoping that things will change at home, or searching his heart for the reasons which made his leaving necessary. Some children, in fact, take refuge in fantasy. The very fact that their parents are inadequate and have "let them down" is denied as being too painful to face and the blame for the family breakdown is put onto the institution, the court or the welfare department. Other children are haunted by fear that it was their own unlovableness that caused their parents to reject them and react with despondency or exaggerated dislike of their own parents, whom still they hope inwardly may someday accept them again. Still others cannot accept the love of anyone else but their own parents, for every kindness shown them points up the contrast with their own homes.

The implications, in fact, of even so simple a fact as the existence of parents in the child's life is tremendous. It means, for instance, that the child coming to the institution today is more "disturbed" than he was in days gone by. He needs more expert and more understanding care and therefore both a better-qualified houseparent and additional staff in the way of social workers and, at least available to the institution, psychologists and psychiatrists. It means that the institution must adapt its program to the possibility of the child's staying under its care for only a part of his child-life. An orphan can be expected to grow up in the institution. A child with parents may go home if his parents recover from illness or change in their ability to care for him. This calls for changes not only in program and organization, but for a much more difficult change than these—that of attitude. The institutional superintendent can no longer be to the same extent the all-sufficient "Daddy" or "Pop" repaid through the life-long devotion of children who have known no other father. His children can no longer be "his" in the same exclusive sense. Rather, more of them will be children whom he has helped over a difficult time in their lives and whom he must then return to other loyalties. Quite obviously this calls for a higher self-discipline and more selfless satisfactions.

It will affect, also, his "public relations" and his institutional pride. There will be fewer loyal alumni who have never known any other home. There may not even be a Children's Home Football Team, the terror of the local league. And the Home's constituency may be less unthinkingly generous. Orphans have an appeal that the children of broken homes do not. The sins of the fathers and mothers are apt to be visited on the children.

But what happens within the institution or how the public looks at it are not by any means the whole of what it means to the institution to have living families for its children. For this very fact presents the institution with a greatly enlarged sphere of service. When parents die there is little that the church can do but care for their children. But when parents are physically, mentally, or socially sick there is much that can be done to restore them to health or, if that is impossible, to help them free their child to find a new family through adoption. Thus the institution ceases to be a service for the child alone. It has to become, if it is to fulfill its full Christian function, a service to the entire family and to be as much concerned with Mrs. Smith's recovery from drinking as with Sally Smith's problem in cheating at school or Tommy's vocational plans and training. The church has no right to care for children apart from their families if they could constructively be together. The ideal of Christianity for the everyday conduct of life is the family, not the convent.

It is all too easy at this point to disclaim responsibility, to throw up one's hands at the unnatural behavior of parents who cannot love a child who seems to us so precious, to want to protect the child from them, condemning them as "bad." It is, of course, possible to do so. One can also all too easily prove one's point by discouraging in parents even the weak little impulses of responsibility and affection they may have. One can make orphans of one's children and in doing so feel like a kindly protector and not what one is, a kidnapper and a Pharisee. One may even find that the results are superficially on one's side. Those children who cannot give up their parents will either rebel against the home and be quietly shifted to state training schools or dismissed as incorrigible. The others will probably conform, be of little trouble to anyone, and in a negative way, do the institution credit. Why this may be undesirable even when it appears to be good must wait for our later discussion of changing values within the church. What is so often forgotten is the plight of the children who cannot conform and the opportunities both conformists and non-conformists have lost for a normal family life. Some families may appear past all helping, but this does not absolve the church of the attempt to save them if it can.

A number of these problems are reinforced, and some new ones presented, by the development during the last twenty or thirty years of alternative methods of child care. When the majority of our older church institutions were founded, in the last quarter of the nineteenth century, they were with few exceptions the only method of caring for children whose homes had broken down. They enjoyed this kind of splendid isolation more or less up to the time of the vast development of public services following the Social Security Act of 1935, although there had been some development of both public aid to children in their own homes and foster family care before that time. Today children in institutions are in a minority. For every child in an institution there are now two in foster-family homes and some 20 receiving public aid on account of the loss of a parent's care and support.

There is no need to fight again the battle of institution *versus* foster home. It was a case of a brash new service, convinced of its own version of the truth and impatient of tradition, struggling with an established service, fearful of competition (and in particular of competition from the state), which had failed to change with the times. The battle was a long and pigheaded one on both sides, and its scars are still with us, in church distrust of secular social work and social work distrust of church organization and motives. It has had the lamentable result of identifying one kind of care (foster-family care) with the state and another (group or institutional care) with the church, so that people value or attack one or the other kind of care not for its intrinsic merits or demerits, but because they are pro- or anti-church. In actual fact, however, far-sighted workers on both sides know that some children, or some children for a part of their child-life, or during the existence of certain problems, need the one kind of care and some the other. The two kinds of care supplement each other, rather than compete; nor, with increasing numbers of children needing care, is there any danger of one form of care squeezing out the other. There was, it is true, a sharp drop in the number of children in institutional care in the first half of this century, but this was due far more to the public support of children in their own homes than to the encroachments of foster-family care. In 1900 many more children were in institutions for reasons of poverty alone—a state of affairs that we are all glad to see remedied.

The concept that children may need group care for a part of their child-life and foster-family care for another part reinforces the problem of adapting the institution to shorter-time service to more children. Children may not only return to their own families but leave institutional care for foster homes, or vice versa. The existence of an alternative kind of care also sharpens the problem of having to care for disturbed or upset children. Not only, as we have seen, are the children who come into any kind of care more disturbed than they used to be because of the nature of their homelessness (to say nothing of the fact that children as a whole are thought by some to be more disturbed), but there is a tendency to refer the more disturbed children of this already disturbed group to the children's institution. This is due to two factors. In the first place it has been shown that many children who are disturbed about their own families can be helped better in group care. In the second, many disturbed children are hard to place in foster homes. Foster-family care, in general, depends on the willingness of normal families to take in, as part of the family, a child who does not belong to it. Boarding rates are low and do little more than cover expenses. The foster parents must find satisfaction in what they can do for the child to be willing to take him in. If the child is too disturbed the difficulties may outweigh the satisfactions and there may be no home for him. While this is not the best of reasons for turning to the institution, it only too often happens, and will while foster-family care remains a more or less volunteer program.

But, more important still, the existence of alternative methods of caring for the homeless child presents the church institution with an entirely new sort of challenge. While its first impulse may be to try to protect itself from what looks like an encroachment on its traditional sphere—a tradition that in any case only goes back some eighty years—more mature thinking focusses on the problem of which children it best can serve and how it can serve them best. This means, first of all, that when it is asked to help a child it must satisfy itself that group care is what the child needs, or perhaps more realistically, that there is no other kind of care that could be made available to him that would better meet his needs.

But this is not the end of the question. It is not simply a question of there being on the one hand the children's institution and on the other foster homes, both immutably set in their ways, geared perhaps to the normal, fairly conforming destitute child. It is not a matter of shrugging one's shoulders and saying, in as many words,

"Well, here we are and over there are foster homes. Which can you use best—or which will do you the least harm?" The real challenge of the alternative is that each kind of care will study the needs of children and what it really has to contribute to them. It means sharpening the tools that each has to work with to meet the need that exists. And in the case of the institution it means a lot of thought about the thing that it has primarily to give and which other facilities cannot offer—the experience of living in a group. What are the values of group living? What children need to live in a group and what children are harmed by it? How can groups be structured to be of the greatest help to children? How big should a living-group be? What mixtures of age, sex, interests, or personality should be included in a group? How can groups both be close enough to be of help to a child and yet not become either cliques or powerful weapons to stifle a child's initiative or his search for his own way of life?

Another problem that the institution has to face, in view of alternative kinds of care, is whether it itself develops these kinds of care. If a child comes to it who needs foster-family care, does the institution refer him to a foster-family care agency or does it itself initiate and maintain a foster-family care program? The answer, of course, will depend on a number of factors. Is there a well-developed foster-family care program to which the child can be referred? Is referral a practical matter or is it too slow to meet needs? Does the institution trust the kind of foster care to which it can refer the child? Is its responsibility for its own constituency such that it cannot entrust the child to another organization—perhaps a secular one? Do family problems demand that a brother, say in the institution and a sister who needs foster-family care need to be cared for by the same agency? (As work with families becomes more sure and is seen to be more important this problem may arise more often.)

Each institution must, of course, find its own answers to these problems. But it cannot avoid them. Nor, except by isolating itself from its community, by refusing to be part of the community's effort for children, can it avoid numerous questions about its relationship to other agencies. What happens, for instance, when a child referred to a public agency needs institutional care? Does the public agency retain responsibility for the child? Who works with the parents? Who pays for the child? The church institution can no longer live to itself, caring only for a favored little flock. It is a part of something bigger in which it can play either a constructive, leading part or a backward, niggling one.

The third thing that has happened to change the task of the institution is that there really have been some discoveries made about the problems of child care. Here I think we have to be careful to distinguish between actual discoveries and changes in fashion or in the kind of character that we aim to turn out. These are, of course, much more matters of opinion. So are some so-called "scientific" discoveries. The question of how strict discipline should be, for example, is in the long run mostly a matter of opinion. Strict discipline produces one kind of character, more permissive handling quite another. You will select the one or the other type of discipline according to which kind of character seems to you the most worthwhile. The question only becomes "scientific" where it can be shown that one kind of discipline or the other produces something that we all recognize as bad, such as mental breakdown, juvenile delinquency, or an inability to hold a job or to live with others—and even these are finally something of value judgments.

There have been, however, certain discoveries about children, and in particular, children away from home, which are more or less universal and do not involve value judgments. If the church does not listen to these it is simply being obstinate and unrealistic. The evidence is all against it and its refusal is on the level of insisting that the earth does not travel round the sun.

Among these discoveries I would list that group care for infants, and indeed for children up to about six years of age, is definitely harmful by any measuring rods that society can devise. It results far too often in a retardation, physical, mental, and emotional, that once firmly established cannot be overcome. While it may still be necessary for us to care for some children under school age in institutions, the only possible reasons for doing this is that we, or other people, have not developed the kind of care that these children really need.

Again, I think that we know with a great deal more sureness the effects that being placed away from home has on most children. This means that not only do we understand better behaviour that formerly seemed to us just "bad" or "ungrateful," but that we know in what area we need to work to overcome it. And a great deal of it is centered in the child's worries about home. We have learned, for instance, that for a parent not to visit does not often result in the child's forgetting him. It is much more likely to cause the child to idealize him and to live in a dream world which prevents his making a satisfactory adjustment in the real one around him. We therefore have become involved with the parent in a new way—not always because we hope for his rehabilitation, not only because we have a feeling for his rights, and certainly not only because we are sentimental about parent and child—but because unless the child is helped to be realistic about his parents he may become very unrealistic indeed, and be almost impossible to help.

Then, too, I think we have learned a good deal more about the effects of long-time institutional care, and especially the kind of institutional care that is insulated from the rest of the community and treats the orphan as a specially favored or specially sheltered individual. It does not matter at this point whether we approve or not of the product of this kind of care. We do know what it is. We know that the "institutional character" which can be produced by this kind of care is conforming, very unlikely to get into serious trouble, often successful by worldly standards, a good follower, but most unlikely to be a leader and generally unable to make any deep relationships in marriage or friendship or to be very creative. While there are many exceptions—what constantly amazes me is the way that some children can with God's help survive and make use of a life which will overwhelm others—the type is common enough for us to want to look at it and determine whether this is what we want.

This raises the problem of values, which I have said seem to be changing within the church itself.

Let us be clear in the first place that this is not a change in ultimate goals. Church institutions have always had a dual goal in the expression of Christian charity, on the part of the donors, and of Christian nurture—to bring up in a Christian environment those who would not otherwise have this opportunity and to provide them with Christian principles on which to live their lives.

Both of these motives still underlie all church child-caring work. But both have, I think, taken on something of a new meaning in this generation. To some these new meanings will not be acceptable. To others, including myself, they represent a deeper understanding of age-old principles, which to me is the essence of conservatism at its best. While there is room for this disagreement it is important, it seems to me, to recognize them as sincere attempts to live up to the Word and not compromises with modern "fashions" or "secularism." If they were that they would indeed be dangerous. I cannot feel that they are.

The greatest change has been in the way in which we help a child acquire Christian principles and live a Christian life. We used to believe—or at least we acted as if we believed—that the surest way to do this was to shelter the child from all the temptations of the world. Thus, for instance, we carefully guarded boys and girls from any but the most formal contacts with each other and from the outside world. (This last was, of course, easier to do when they were orphans without family ties.) The "institutional character" with its conformity and its shallowness was more or less our ideal. It was on the whole a negative ideal. It put very little trust in man's capacity to choose good for himself, and put most of its reliance on his environment and training "to keep him good."

While no one would doubt that children need some protection

from the temptations of life, I think to many people the concept of Christian living has been deepened. They see a Christian not as a person who lives apart from the world, but one who lives in it by Christian principles; not one who is sheltered from temptation but one who meets it successfully. Partly by circumstances, therefore, but even more by conviction, good church institutions have become much more part of the world around them. All that happens to a child no longer takes place within the institution's walls. He goes to school in the public schools, joins a Scout troop in the community, visits back and forth with friends who live in their own homes and is far less "set aside" than he used to be. This is not a compromise with the world but a desire to transform it in a Christian way rather than flee from it. Perhaps this is more risky, but the Christian life has never been a safe one. It is far more realistic and it promises far more to society—a living, active Christianity that transforms the world rather than a negative one which operates outside it. You may, of course, disagree with me here. We could both adduce good texts to prove our point. But at least this is what many good Christians now believe.

Along with this change there has gone at least the beginnings of a new attitude toward Christian charity and the objects of it. One of the greatest dangers of charity—even Christian charity—is that it should lose sight of its real nature—responding to God's overwhelming love by "loving one's neighbor as oneself"—and become something we do to confirm us in our belief in our own goodness, or even to accumulate in some way "merit" for ourselves. As long as we look on children in institutions as objects of pity, as "other people's children" to whom we are being generous, charity can so easily slide into condescension or be used to expiate our own guilt for our undeserved good fortune. What has been developing, however, and what needs to be developed is not pity but the sense of Christian responsibility—the determination that other people shall share in the good fortune we have from God. These then become "our children"—part of our church and our community—and what we want for them is what we would want for our own children, no more and no less. And this kind of responsibility is not easily developed. None of the real Christian virtues are arrived at easily.

The net result, then, of all these changes has been to transform the church institution, to present it with challenges and responsibilities that before it never dreamed of, and at the same time to offer it the opportunity of service of a far wider sort than it traditionally has had. We are gathered together today to consider some of these challenges, in all humility, asking that the Lord guide us and prevent us from the mistake of ever thinking that we know or ever can know all the answers to the problems that He has faced us with.

2

The Christian Challenge of the Children's Home*

IN A NUMBER OF Southern children's homes I am known as a story-teller—no, not of fibs but of some of the most beloved heroes of our Southland, Brer Rabbit, Brer Possum and the rest. Thus it seems right that I should start by telling you two stories tonight, not indeed from Uncle Remus but about your children's homes and the change that has taken place in them, so confusing if you do not understand why and where and how, and so exciting if you do.

This then is the first story. Once upon a time there was a boy and a girl, call them Billy and Alice, whose mother and father died of pneumonia, and who were sent to an orphanage built and sup-ported by their church. There they learned good manners, a great deal about the Bible, not to drink or smoke, and some very good work habits—better ones, in fact, than most people feel it necessary to acquire, because they were orphans and would have a hard row to hoe in the world. And there they lived in a big building with forty other boys and girls, and were looked after as far as their physical wants were concerned by the kind widow of a minister who was herself alone in the world and for whom the church had provided a job.

She did not find them beyond her powers, for Billy and Alice were grateful children and cooperated well. Why should they not? This was the only home that they had and they were very conscious of how kind the church had been. It was true, of course, that they were somewhat different. They didn't have things of their own or go to school with other children or have the fun that others did, but being orphans they did not expect it and took instead the parties that the kind church people gave them. And in time they graduated from the orphanage school as model citizens and a credit to their church. It is true that they found it a little difficult to adjust them-selves to a real world; that not many of them showed very much initiative—they were better servants than masters, better followers than leaders—and that some of them found some difficulty in form-ing any very deep relationships in life. But this was hardly to be

* Originally given as a talk to the Baptist Brotherhood of a church in Lakeland, Fla., September 1958. Reprinted in *Charity and Children*, May 12, 19 and June 2, 1960, and in shortened form under the title "What You Should Know of Orphans and Orphanages" in *Presbyterian Survey*, May 1960.

expected of them and the church could well feel satisfied with what it had done.

Now this is a very nice little story—once upon a time. There is only one catch to it. It happened forty-five years ago, in 1914 to be exact. And yet there are hundreds of thousands of sincere, intelligent people who expect it to happen just like that in 1959, and think that there must be something wrong with their children's home if it does not. These same people would never dream of conducting their businesses on 1914 lines, with pre-World War I advertising, pre-machine age products, pre-inflation wage scales. Maybe of course they would like to—who does not long sometimes for the good old days?—but no businessman in his senses would set out today to manufacture buggy-whips by candlelight and sell them from a huckster's stand.

So now let us look at our second story. We may not like it. We may wish that it didn't have to be this way. But we cannot avoid it. This is what happens today.

Gary and Debbie, our modern children, have parents who are still alive. One does not die of pneumonia now, not in one's child-rearing years. Less than one in thirty of the Garys and Debbies who need us now are orphans in the old sense.

But Gary and Debbie still need us. Their parents are sick, perhaps physically, more likely mentally, for whether we like it or not this is the prevalent disease. Or, more likely, their parents are half sinners and half sick, and no one knows exactly how much the one and how much the other. To Gary and Debbie it does not matter. What they know is that adults cannot be trusted, that somehow they always let you down. So Gary and Debbie are distrustful, disturbed, perhaps pre-delinquent. And then one of two things happens. Either their parents give up the struggle, send them to a home or desert them, or society steps in and Gary and Debbie are removed from their sick home.

Now Billie and Alice, our first children, were grateful to their church. They needed a home and the church gave one. But Gary and Debbie have a home. It is true that it is not a very good one, but it is all that they have known. Why, then, they ask themselves, do they have to leave it?

Because their parents do not love them? Can you see what it would mean to have to admit that? To a child it means nearly always, deep down in the heart, "because there is something wrong with me, because I'm not worthy to be loved." And so children will try to find any other reason that makes sense. And the most frequent is, "because people (and these church people most of all) do not understand the situation; because they interfered. And therefore I must try to fight them. I must not accept their love." I remember one Debbie who told me so in so many words. Here she was, a bright seven-year-old blonde who had been removed from a hopelessly feeble-minded mother, from a home where she had foraged for her meals in garbage cans. Yet this Debbie was not grateful. Instead she had developed a perfectly devilish ability to find the weak link in the armor of anyone who tried to love her. She became literally unmanageable.

Finally in desperation I was called in to see the child, and, as we talked together we were looking at a coloring book. Debbie stopped for a moment at a picture of Baby Bunting in his cradle up a tree and, caught unawares a moment, said in the saddest voice, "You know, that mother left that baby up a tree." This was her real, her secret fear, her inside knowledge of what had happened to her. But when I asked her what the baby thought about it, Debbie whirled on me. "It's a lie, a lie," she shouted. "Some robbers and murderers took that child away from home." However much we loved Debbie, we were robbers and murderers to her. Quite apart from the kind of disturbance Debbie showed as a result of years of neglect, she added to it another, more desperate kind.

Perhaps the children's home tries to keep Debbie's mother away from her, as in fact they had quite understandably done in this case. It would be good if Debbie could forget, have a new start in life. Besides, why should such a terrible mother be allowed to see the child she has starved, or beaten, or neglected for drink or lust? But this does not help Debbie at all. In fact, what the Garys and Debbies do if they cannot see their parents is to build up in their minds an unreal picture of what mother is like. She becomes idealized and they are even more disgruntled because they are kept away from home.

So for Gary and Debbie's sake the home works with the parents, even the sick and terrible parents. And then they discover a new challenge about which I would like to talk awhile.

When the home took Billy and Alice in those far-off days, that was the end of the matter. One cannot undo Death. But when Gary and Debbie come, their parents are sick; they are not dead. Can the church remain complacent before a broken family? Can it, a saving agency, write people off as hopeless sinners and not try to find the divine spark which is present, somewhere, in every man? Must it not put out every effort to save the family if it can? The job of the home is widened then from that of caring for children to that of saving families—and this is quite a different job. It means, for instance, that we no longer take Garys and Debbies and hope to keep them until they are grown. It means that we have a higher ideal— to return them whole and cured to a family that also has learned to be one again.

So now we have three brand new problems that the old orphanage never had—the disturbed and distrustful child, the one who will not be staying with us but whom we must help for a short time, and the need to work with parents both to help disturbed children while they are with us, and because we know in our heart of hearts that family life is the Christian ideal. And all these three problems are only accentuated by one more shift in the world—the growth of foster family care and adoption programs.

It is no part of my business tonight to discuss these programs in themselves, although they are also exciting and challenging. And far less is it my business to defend institutional care from the imagined inroads of what some misguided people think of as rivals instead of most welcome and useful allies. But these programs have had their effect on the children's homes. For instance, although some people still like to argue about which is the "best" kind of care, we know that in actual fact some children need one and some the other, and some need first the one and then the other at different times. And we know that in general the long-time dependent child, the orphan, and in particular the less damaged child—the one you can point to with pride as the product of your care—does best in a foster home or can be found a new family in adoption. And, by the same token, the child who needs short-time care, the child who has strong family ties, either of love, or, strangely enough, of hate, the child who is most disturbed and most difficult, is the one that needs the children's home most. So there is no relief here—only a bigger problem and a more exciting challenge.

The burden of this change and this challenge falls both on those of you who have been called to serve in the children's home and on you other thousands who support it and make it possible. If I dwell first on what these mean to the children's home itself, it is only because in order for you to do your part you need to understand what is involved there. I shall come to your part in time, and I warn you, it won't be easy for you, either, although what you are called on to do will be most certainly worthwhile.

For the institution it means principally three things. It means first *a better and a more highly trained and diversified staff* to cope with much more difficult children. It means houseparents who have a real call for their job—not matrons who are themselves the objects of charity. It means training for houseparents, on and off the campus. It means trained social workers who are skilled in working with difficult families. It means part time at least the help of psychiatrists and psychologists, for the church cannot afford to ignore the skills of science, although it must always offer them the leadership of its spirit and use them in a Christian way.

It means, also, *the sharpening of all the tools that the institution has to be of help to children,* and in particular that tool which the institution uniquely has, the tool of living together in groups. And this means smaller units, ten or twelve children in a cottage instead of the thirty or forty for which the cottage, perhaps, was built. It means not calculating how many children one housemother can possibly clothe and feed and discipline, but how many children can profitably share one housemother's love and care. It means too courageous thinking about the composition of groups—which children shall live together and how and why and where. It means individualization within a group structure and not mass handling.

And thirdly it means *a program to prepare children for the return to normal life*—not as a special class of "orphans" but as everyday citizens. And this means in fact a revision of our whole idea of what constitutes a Christian education, not to make it less Christian but to make it more truly education. It means bringing up children in a real world, encouraging them in community activities, sending them to public schools. It means not sheltering them from temptation so much as helping them to withstand temptation; not bringing them up a group untouched by the world but as a group that will transform the world. It means programs adapted to a changing population and learning how to help here and now, not only in the long pull.

But Homes will not be able to do the work they need to do unless you people do your part. And your part is not an easy one. It calls for real religious discipline. For although your task is the same as it has always been—to interpret, to understand, to support, to approve, to guide in general—your faith will be tested in four most rigorous ways.

First, at a time when your children need you perhaps as they have never needed you before, *there will be less obvious things to be proud of.* It will become harder and harder to point to a model citizen and say, "He was raised in our Church Home." You are much more likely to find a man or a woman who is making a go of things despite a family background or a set of disasters which would normally be crushing and say, "We helped him in his hour of greatest need. That he has come through at all is partly due to us. He may not know it, but we did our part." And at the same time there will be, as the years go on, less possibility of many very pleasant things to which we used to point with pride, such as orphanage football teams (the erstwhile terrors of the league now merged in public school activities), homecoming days and chances to see how well our children sing hymns or behave on a picnic—not that many of them don't, but that it is, to me at least, amazing that some of these children can come up even to everyday standards, so troubled have they been and are.

Then, *you are going to get less visible results for your money and yet be asked to give more.* The job is vastly more difficult than it was forty years ago. You are not just caring for children—not just educating them, giving them a Christian home—but all this and a great deal more. You are repairing broken lives. It costs much more to repair a church than to keep it in running order, but the observer sees only that the church is in moderately good shape. It costs money for good staff, for smaller groups, for services.

It may and will hurt your good business sense to see a building with a cubic foot capacity big enough for forty children lived in by ten or twelve—unless, of course, you understand why this must be. You can see groups of well-behaved children deployed on an orphanage lawn. You can't see a mended heart or even, for the most part, a re-united family. You can see on paper at least a rising per capita cost but not what this rising cost has bought.

Again, *you are going to have to wrestle with less comfortable emotions.* Orphans are easy to give to; they pluck at the heartstrings, they give returns in gratitude. Disturbed children are much harder. They ask of you a more mature, less selfish love. The work of the church will not go forward unless in every congregation pity (which is all to often at bottom a selfish emotion) flies out of the window and stewardship and Christian responsibility take its place, And this is going to be doubly hard because such is sinful man that he would rather give from pity than from stewardship.

And lastly, *you are going to have to make up your mind to help in distasteful circumstances.* Many of the children who now demand your help bring with them memories of things we all would rather forget but cannot: rape, alcoholism, desertion, incest, murder. Many of the parents whom we must help for the children's sake have been guilty of these or of many lesser things. There are just as many children who call to you as there ever have been, but they need you for a different, less acceptable reason than did the orphans of yesteryear. And if we are to help them, we must have the courage to face the truth and the loving-kindness to work with those whose crimes hurt us but whom we do not dare condemn while there is a chance that they can learn to change.

These are hard words, but this is the Christian challenge, which was never presented to man as an easy thing. You and thousands like you have a big decision to make. You can accept the challenge or you can decide that it is too difficult for you. You can help build a social service that is worthy of the church, that witnesses to its leadership in the world, or you can, as churches have too often done in the past, refuse the challenge, withdraw from the field, or hope that in some way you can muddle through with the old tools. You can pretend to yourselves that piety, which must be the cornerstone of any building, will also serve as bricks and mortar, which in fact it won't. Without piety a house will fall, but piety is not enough. Other things are needed to build on it—knowledge, and courage, and common sense.

You can, in fact, declare that the church wishes to abdicate its leadership in the social service field, as it already has to some extent, and leave everything to the secular arm. But if you do so, you will do so at a time when I think that there are clearer signs than at any time within the past half-century that the church's leadership is needed. The church will never again be the sole social agency, and this, I think, is right. It will never again be the biggest one. The state will always have the greater resources and in our modern society the obligation to meet the greatest part of the need. But the church does, in my humble opinion, have the right, the opportunity, and the obligation to provide leadership, to be on "the growing edge" of the effort to meet the problems of human need. This is in fact its destiny which it can take up or refuse.

3.

Whither?*

FIRST I WOULD LIKE to make known my conviction about the
genuineness of the advance in this work since 1950. This has been
truly exciting and is, I think, beginning to write itself on the national
picture and to disturb conventional thinking both about institutions
and about the contribution of the Church to social welfare. Of
course, this advance did not start in 1950. It was already underway.
But this has been a significant decade, and of one thing I am sure.
It is not the kind of growth of the seed which, in the parable, fell in
shallow ground and flourished exceedingly for a while before it
withered away. It is a growth that has deep roots in three qualities,
at least, that I recognize in this group. It is rooted, first, in a genuine
concern for people—not for children alone, much as you may love
them, but for parents, and houseparents, for saints and sinners alike
—which transcends selfish interests and narrow moralisms. It is
rooted, secondly, in a willingness to learn, in a Christian humility, in
a refusal to accede to the modern illusion that the expert or the long
time practitioner can ever know all there is to know about a program
or a person. And thirdly it is rooted in a genuine conservatism—a
willingness to adapt rather than to destroy, to test out rather than to
improvise, and a deep sense of a tradition that goes back far beyond
the foundation of your particular institutions or even of your denomi-
nations to the sources of Christian and western culture.

In this kind of soil what kind of a flowering can you expect?
We have to take weather into account, and a weather prophet is
notoriously inaccurate. But I do not think there is any doubt that
the weather ahead is changeable. Something is happening in our
culture that is of tremendous importance. Most of us are by now
accustomed to thinking of this age as one of disintegration, of conflict
and tension, and to a certain extent this will continue to be true. But
there is growing a new problem of a somewhat different nature. It
looks as if the sixties will be not so much the anxious age but the age
of shallowness, the age of "I don't care," the age of "why worry?",
the age of non-commitment, of lack of purpose, of emptiness. How
far this will go I do not know. It is already beginning to be the
cultural pattern of today—the culture of the lonely crowd, the Beat-
nik or the aimless delinquent. One recent writer goes so far as to

* A "prophetic" paper given to The Southeastern Child Care Association
at its fifty-fifth annual meeting, Savannah, Ga., April 7, 1960, and reprinted in
Connie Maxwell, Summer 1960.

suggest that the content of man's unconscious mind has changed, that we repress today not our hostility, not our dangerous impulses, but all the things that used to challenge us to a more meaningful life.

Now in any such age of breakdown there is always in the social fabric a growing-point, the beginning, as it were, of the age after that. Ages do not simply stop and begin. They overlap. Just as in the age of the dinosaur when these tremendously powerful forms—they had lasted a million years—came to an end the hitherto unimportant mammals provided the growing point for a new advance, so, on a far lesser scale, in the social welfare field today it is not inconceivable that this growing point—this herald of the age to be—may be the church-related, although not necessarily the church-sponsored, facility.

This may sound like an incredible thing to say about a type of child-care that has so often been discounted and that received, for instance, exactly one sentence in a recent 56-page report on North Carolina's children. I make it, however, because if what I have said about the age is true—that it is an age whose major problem is that it lacks content and purpose—then secular social science will not be able to fill the gap. Psychiatry, secular social work, sociology as we know it, have made a tremendous contribution to personality in the past because their principal purpose has been to unshackle, to disentangle, to set free. They were the growing-point of the last period of standstill thirty to fifty years ago, when the moralistic attitudes of the church proved inadequate to a new and exciting world. They are still important to us. But by themselves they are inadequate to provide what the world so desperately needs—a content and a purpose for living. For this they need revitalizing from an older set of insights. And as I look round the field today the one place where the new knowledge and the older insights appear to be working together is among agencies such as yours.

So I am putting my eggs in this basket; but I do not mean to suggest for a moment that the future is automatically ours. It is not something that we can complacently wait for. The mammals did not supersede the saurians without growth and development on their part. But I think that there are signs that there is something here if we can only catch hold of it. For instance, a recent study of all kinds of child-caring facilities emphasizes a virtual breakdown in attempts to work with parents and re-establish family life, and yet, I believe, you have in general learned and done a great deal about this in the last few years.

What kind of a future can we see then for the institution? For better or worse I will make a few guesses, each one predicated of your willingness to meet this challenge. I do not think I need to say that the opportunity could be lost, that our worst enemies are ourselves,

our own lack of imagination, our retreat at the first cold winds of
spring.

First, I see the kind of agency that you represent becoming
gradually more important in the whole scheme of things. For a time
this may be a slow development. But in twenty or thirty years, or
maybe much sooner or later— the chief error of prophets, weather
prophets or biblical prophets, has always been that their timing is
off—I can see the development of what might be called a third force,
alongside and on a par with the public welfare departments and the
community-fund highly professional counselling services, which will
be denominational or interdenominational. I would even suggest that
this may be a new and important type of agency which will be recognized as specifically American, just as our public welfare agencies are
at the moment perhaps our most typical American contribution to
the social welfare of the world. And I would hazard that its beginning may come out of the South.

This agency will be highly complex. It will offer a number of
services, or, if it does not, it will be part of a network of services
among which there will be much interchange. For one thing, the
long established dichotomy between institutional and foster family
care will have broken down. In its place there will be a continuum
of services, from the more or less natural family setting, through the
subsidized foster home and the off-campus cottage to what most of
us have today, into each of which children can be steered as their
needs change or their ability to relate is enhanced. Yet the agency
will not become large and sprawling. It will be tightly held together
in a clear-cut structure and a common core of beliefs.

This agency will be more professional than it has been in the
past, but it will not belong to one profession, nor will it merely borrow
or buy professional skill from the outside. It will have in it, as part
of its total structure, social workers, child-care workers, educators,
artists, doctors, business men, and pastors, each the best that it can
find, each with his contribution to make, but each owing allegiance
to a view of man that will be more or less explicit. It will have to
train these men and women not, I think, within itself, for they will
need the insights of a wider world, but through encouragement and
material help to those whom it will need.

It will stand for something. This is no time for the relativist, for
the assumption that all values are equally good. That is why we are
in this impasse. But it will not, as its predecessors, see life largely in
terms of what to avoid. I think that what it will stand for really is
the meaning of people to each other, of parent to child and child to
parent and husband to wife and wife to husband. It will truly be
a place in which children and parents learn to trust others and themselves. As such it will be concerned not so much in helping people

adjust to life as in filling this life with content. This may mean a new emphasis on program, on richer experience, on trust and love and fun. For the modern "disturbed" child is no longer in conflict as much as he was. He is what the psychiatrists call "ego-deficient," without the ability to discriminate or care about what he does. So the house mother's job may become even more important than it is today, and the social worker's not so much one of solving problems but of engaging parent and child more fully in all that the institution can give.

All this is not going to happen tomorrow, or the day after that. What will the next year or two hold? Where do we go from here?

These are much harder questions to answer. But essentially they are of the same sort. What, I would say to you, will be important tomorrow—and are important today—are the steps that we can take at this time towards being the kind of agency on which the future can build. And although we may all have our ideas as to what these might be I would suggest, quite tentatively, that the following may have importance:

(1) Efforts to enrich the daily life of our children, not so much in material things, but in contacts with worthwhile people and in learning and activity that challenges rather than occupies.

(2) Efforts to find a way of life that may be fuller of trust and love and in many ways more demonstrative of it, than we often have at present where we seem so much concerned with order and control.

(3) Efforts to find more meaningful ways of involving parents in their children's lives, including attention to such apparently obvious things such as family conferences, agreements, and procedures whereby children move in and out.

(4) Efforts to find a structure that will give each profession support, status, and a defined place in institutional life. This means, for instance, more thought about supervision, and more careful definition of what a social worker, a pastor or a superintendent does.

(5) Continuing efforts to recruit and train staff of the highest quality both of knowledge and richness of personality. The institution of the future will be able to afford neither the denying houseparent nor the unimaginative social worker nor the pastor with a fuzzy theology.

(6) Wise experimentation with what we have in the areas, for instance, of cottage groupings, off-campus cottages, special classes, work and recreational programs.

(7) A new emphasis on imaginative research into what constitutes good content, good procedure, good organization, and good relationships in the field.

4.

The Role of the Institution in the Sixties*

WHEN I AM ASKED to talk about the role of this or that social service, or this or that kind of agency, an uncomfortable picture comes to my mind. This is that of the Utopian society, in which there has been created a complicated and interlocking network of social services to meet every conceivable human need, and in which public and private agencies, institutions and foster homes, day care centers and homemaker services, Catholics, Baptists, and Holy Rollers, each play their assigned and definable role. This is the dream, or perhaps should I say nightmare, of the social scientist, the planner, and I do not like the idea at all.

Of course there are ways in which social agencies should work together and try to avoid unnecessary duplication, or should agree between themselves not leave uncovered too glaring a human need. Of course there is virtue in having in any state, or community, or church a well-rounded or even a comprehensive program, well-designed and equitable. But the kind of picture which I have painted in which everyone has his assigned role is to my mind presumptuous, the sort of thing which God delights in permitting the Devil to use to chasten humanity and turn into an instrument of sterility and social control. Besides, it is simply not the way in which what we know as progress works. Progress, real progress, the new idea, the sudden break-through, rarely comes from the refinement of what served us well in the past. It comes from unexpected quarters, from what the Bible calls a remnant. When the dinosaurs came to an end a remnant was found in the unconsidered and apparently ill-equipped mammals. When Greek and Roman civilization crumbled a remnant was found in a sect that had been at first quite out of touch with the values of the civilization whose memory it was part of its glory to keep alive. Any society, indeed, needs its independents, its people who do not quite fit in with the established order of things. It is these who provide the new beginning when the old becomes too refined, too complicated or too sure of itself.

I may be quite at fault in suggesting that the present potential of the children's institution to play its part in the social services of the country is due to some extent to the fact that it has not become part of a sociologist's dream. I may be wrong in my belief that

* Given to the Southwestern Regional Workshops for Personnel in Children's Institutions, Austin, Texas, June 1961.

some of the real break-throughs are coming in this field. But I shudder to think what would have happened if institutions had accepted the role assigned to them by the social thinkers of the 1930's and 1940's. They would have become, in fact, a necessary and dwindling evil, a dumping ground for those children whom society did as yet not know how to treat, a waste-paper basket for the reject. They would have dissipated their strength. I can find it in my heart to be thankful that some of them were so obdurate about it; even that some were pig-headed and continued with practices that even they, I think, sometimes knew to be wrong.

And even now that institutions are respectable again, I would call on them not to accept too readily roles assigned to them by the social thinkers of today. It is not that I think that these roles are wrong, but that I believe most strongly roles must be created out of the past, out of what is there, out of what a service is like and not assigned by outsiders. Social welfare is not a play with a director, except for God Himself, and He is inclined to use us for purposes of which we may be only dimly aware at the time. Thus, when the social scientists say that the children's institution should become a treatment center, clinically oriented, staffed with psychiatrists and psychiatric counsellors, I would say yes, some may want to become exactly that. There is certainly a need for more and better treatment centers, and all honor is due to those who voluntarily and with conviction take on this expensive and difficult task. But there are also other ways in which an institution can develop, and some of these, I am sure, are as yet undreamed and undiscovered. I myself had no idea five years ago of the way in which some institutions would be able to use their structure to enable parents and children to make a new start in their family relationships. Yet more than one children's institution is today doing exciting work in this field of practice. I was not sure a few years ago that the experience of group living could be used, not only negatively to protect an injured child, but positively to restore to him trust lost in adults, in himself, and in the Providence of God, but institutions I have worked with have shown me that this is indeed possible. I was not aware, although perhaps I had some inklings of this, of how much the foster family field would find itself needing in 1961 to learn or to re-learn some of the basic principles that institutions had long been held to, such as agency responsibility and the importance of being there to help the child.

But institutions have not survived, and do not have a great potential in the years to come, because they were right and others wrong, or because there is any magic in the kind of care they provide. I want to make that very clear. Indeed many of them have been from time to time quite horribly wrong, and some have been cruel and blind and haphazard. They have survived and have an important role to play in the future only because those who run them have learned to use what they are in a constructive way. What they are has in fact led to two very important virtues of which the child welfare field stands greatly in need. But first, people had to use these characteristics for good and not for ill, and they could have been used either way.

The first of these virtues is a feeling of responsibility and concern for every child. The very fact that the institution cares for children within its walls and that its staff sees and talks with them daily has enabled it to see more clearly, once its eyes were opened to the fact that a child away from home needs a great deal more than a favorable environment. Foster family care, although it knows better, is always subject to the temptation under the pressure of work, or because it would be nice if it were true, to think that it has done its job when it has found the child a home, and not to be too concerned with planning, or working out family relationships or even really knowing how the child is thinking and feeling, from that time on. Indeed, although at one time the institution was full of "forgotten" children for whom no one was too deeply concerned except when they caused trouble, it is probably true today that there are fewer forgotten children in the institution than there are in other forms of care. And when the institution itself turns to foster family care to supplement its program some of this care and concern and need for planning has become apparent in the foster family program. Foster parents are seen more clearly as responsible associates of the agency for which they work, instead of unrelated people with whom one "places" a child, and frequent transfers or their equally deadly opposite, long-term plans that lead nowhere, become less frequent.

The second quality that has enabled the institution to change and grow is in part a result of the very qualities for which it has been most criticized—its isolation from the community and its not being a natural kind of care, but rather an "artificial" one. For these have made it in a way more able to experiment and less dependent on the network of relationships in community life. These have enabled it to try out different kinds of grouping, different and varied programs for children, special services that are not possible in the normal or natural community. Please do not misunderstand me here. I am not going back on the lesson that we have been learning for years, that an institution must be part of the community in which it is set. We are not interested in being little islands shut away from the outside world. But let us realize that there is a kind of flexibility possible because of our very difference; that there are things one can do for children within an institution's walls that are not possible in a private home, from ignoring certain kinds of behavior that we could not allow in a private home to permitting children to form relationships with a variety of people to changes of pace or pressure in day-to-day living.

So it all comes back to the way in which the institution is used. For these very same factors—the institution's concern for children and its artificiality, its difference from ordinary living, which have enabled it to contribute so greatly to the child welfare field are at the same time the source of its greatest temptations. Care and concern for children, one of its greatest strengths, can and does result too often in an overprotectiveness, a desire to shield children from the realities of life, to watch them, to chaperone them and even to indulge them at the cost of their ability to make their own choices in life. We still have a good deal to do in improving ourselves here. Overprotectiveness is always much easier than letting a child grow up. And the very fact of our difference, of our being something constructed and not natural in the community, can lead and has led all too often to institutional pride, to an interest in product rather than in true helping, and to a tendency to reject the child who does not conform to what we think he ought to be.

An institution is in fact rarely good or bad in itself. It is not a machine, either, with a precise form that can only be used to perform an assigned function and is useless for everything else. It is rather a way of caring for children that has certain characteristics which can be used wisely or unwisely, with love and understanding or with pride and indifference. I am reminded very vividly of an institution I visited recently. In one sense everything was wrong—isolated position, little or no community contacts, both school and church on the campus, the sort of cottage one could never use for anything but a strict peer-group kind of living, no professional staff, and a budget that would not stand any real expansion of service. And here I was, being asked to tell them what their role should be—a thing that I found a number of people had been doing all along. I thought of all the obvious answers: treatment center—far too expensive and no access to a psychiatrist; adolescents—their adolescents were feeling more than most their isolation from the community; large families—they were breaking up families by the very way that they lived in four age and sex groups; family rehabilitation—they were too inaccessible to work unusually well with parents. I almost felt like saying, "Scrap it, and let's begin all over again." And yet there was something that felt right about what they were doing. There was a relaxed air on campus, a very low incidence of punishment, a lack of pressure or pace. As a wise state consultant had put it. "You do everything wrong, but somehow it works." And quite suddenly I saw, or at least I hope I saw, what it was they had to contribute. This institution had a very real gift with the awkward

child, the slow learner, the ugly duckling, the uncouth and the un-
tutored, the child who as yet had little to give in return to foster
parents or who would find the competition in the public schools too
much to take. So I recommended to them that they study whether
they could not specialize in children such as these; whether they
could not turn the handicap of a school on the premises (the community schools could not take them) into an asset and use it to help
these children catch up a little. At the same time I did try to hold
them to certain things that they plainly needed, such as someone
to work with parents and a more flexible cottage set-up. As I write
I am afraid it sounds as if it was I who made these decisions but I
do not think that it was so. I hope that what I really did was to
help them discover themselves.

This is, in fact, what I would want to say to institutions about
their role in the 1960's—that it may be any one of a number of
things, but that what is really important is that it takes advantage
of what an institution is, that it be purposeful, and that it build on a
particular institution's strengths and even its limitations. The institution needs to be much more than just a place to rear children. It
needs to discover what it can do well and do it with all the skill it
can muster, and it needs to be able to change and do something different when needs change or new discoveries about what can be
done are made. It needs to take every advantage of sound professional training and knowledge in house staff as well as pro-
fessionals, in its pastor as well as its social worker. It cannot afford
to be second-rate, only natural things like families can afford to be
that. When it is a church institution, it would be my feeling that
it should clearly and unequivocably witness to some important aspect
of the Christian gospel, such as the church's redemptive purpose and
its belief in the possibility of grace even for the most unlikely, or
the church's special love for the handicapped or unlovely, in the
words of a hymn remembered from childhood.

> Love to the loveless shown
> That they may lovely be.

It should not be doing the sort of job that other agencies can do just
as well or better. It should not be just another agency, caring for
a few extra children, the overflow as it were. There are times, of
course, when it may have to do this for a while, but this should not
be its goal. It is more than a cog in the wheel.

Of course if the institution is part of the state or of local government, it may find its role pretty well assigned to it. It may have
to be a detention home, or a training facility for delinquent boys or
girls. But even there it seems to me that it needs to study carefully
what it can do with what it has, and what new ways it can find to

use its group nature and the fact of its difference. It can at least make explicit whom it can serve best, and why, and what other facilities are needed to serve the children it has. And above all it can experiment with groupings and with aspects of its program. The whole question, for instance, of the involvement of the parent in the work of the state home for delinquents is a virtually untouched field, but where it has been touched it has paid dividends.

This, in fact, is the kind of role that I would suggest for the children's institution in the 1960's—that it should recognize a paradox that the institution, which seems so unchangeable in terms of bricks and mortar, is actually the most flexible of all methods of child care. The foster home changes only with the culture in which it is set and the quality of the people that it employs. The institution, because it is a subculture of its own, can, while keeping its roots in the prevailing culture, yet create new forms of care, which may be one of the reasons why this field has been so exciting in the last ten or fifteen years. Of course, this depends on people, too, on the kind of people you are, and the people you employ. For the institution must pay the price of any man-made tool. Like gunpowder or like atomic energy it can be used to advance knowledge or good living, or it can be used to destroy them.

Thus I would say to you insofar as you remain true to yourselves and study diligently the kind of tool you have in your hands, inasmuch as you maintain at least in part your independence, insofar as you tackle your problems with a desire to learn and not with a sense that you have the answers, and inasmuch as you recognize that we are only at the beginning of this business of child care, you will find your role, or be called to it, rather than have it assigned to you.

5.

The Intangible Needs of Group Living*

THE ONE THING which an institution offers uniquely to a child is the experience of living in a group, artificially constructed specifically to meet his needs. Other people live in groups—students, servicemen, the religious—but in their case the group usually has some outside purpose to which it is incidental; and of course all of us live in and out of groups, in our homes (the family group), at work, at worship, and in play. But generally these are voluntary, and in any case we move rapidly from one to another, or withdraw from all for a time. Only the institutional child is part of the same group necessarily and inevitably the greater part of the day and night.

Group living has often been criticized, because it is unnatural, because it fails to provide the close one-to-one relationship which we know is ordained as man's most precious experience, in marriage, in parenthood, in prayer. Group living is described sometimes as empty, impersonal, lacking in warmth. It has been held to produce an unimaginative conformity and to demand of its members that they surrender their individuality.

All these are justified criticisms. Group living can be exactly this. It is, if it is not used wisely. But this criticism ignores the other side of the picture, the fact that group-living does have a great deal to offer to certain children with certain needs, and that at any one time these needs may be uppermost in a person's life.

Man is in fact both a social and an individual person. He needs and wants both to be treated the same as every one else and differently from them, just as he needs, for instance, both private prayer and corporate worship. Group living can become a marvellously delicate instrument to help those who have found the one-to-one relationship with their fellow men too demanding or even destructive. This includes many children in whom the one-to-one relationship most open to a child, the parent-child relationship, has been up to now disastrous. To these children group living can offer two im-

* Given at the Third Annual Workshop for Personnel of Homes for Children, Austin, Texas, June 1961.

portant values. It can offer what we call security, that is, a predictable, sure world where one is not naked and alone nor does one have to pit one's strength against events too big for one, and it can offer freedom of choice, the chance to rebuild relationship at one's own pace and to some extent with whom one will.

It *can* offer these values. It does not always do so. Nor is it permissible to offer one value and not the other, except when a child's need is very one-sided, for they are the two sides of a coin. As some of you know, I have spent quite a bit of my time these last few years studying groups in institutions and making diagrams of them. I have seen groups that were all security and no freedom in relationship, and too much security kills the spirit. I have seen groups where children had to pick up relationship where they could, and these were as cruel as the jungle and about as satisfying. But I have also seen many good and useful groups.

This is not all a matter of how the group is constituted. A great deal of the usefulness of group living depends on the way that the living-group is related to other groups on campus and the way in which the individual is helped to operate in the group. It is largely a matter of balance, of being able to give to a child all the advantages of being part of a group and yet retain for him his uniqueness as a person. And so I would like to sketch for you eight needs which I believe are common to all children in group-care which really make it possible for the child to gain from the experience. In fact I would suggest that you might from time to time look at any one child and ask if these needs are being met. If they are not, perhaps you ought to do something about it. And perhaps you ought to consider whether what needs to be changed is the child, who may be either in the wrong group or in the wrong kind of care, or whose attitudes may be hurting him, or the group itself, which may need re-adjusting or even re-constituting, or the part that you as house-parents or executives are playing in it. I do not pretend, of course, that this is an inclusive list but it may do as a beginning. It does exclude a whole lot of needs which are common to all children, like love and limits and understanding, and needs of children which are common to children away from home, such as support and help with one's negative feelings. These are simply the needs that are specific to the use of a group.

First then is the *need to be included if one wants in, but only then.* Some children are too distrustful, and sometimes justifiably so, to be able to make relationships quickly or even ever very deeply, and some of these feel safer in a group than on their own. But there is all the difference in the world between what we call a "voluntary isolate"—the child who holds himself out of the group— and the child who is rejected by it. What this means in fact is that the group must not be dominated by an exclusive "gang" or "clique" that cannot admit newcomers or anyone else but themselves, and even makes it impossible for sub-groupings to be formed. For a child does not need necessarily to be part of the in-group, the clique that has the greatest status, but he does need to have a chance to belong to *some* group in the cottage, even if it is originally what I call "a company of misery," a grouping of those left out. It is strange, incidentally, how such a sub-group can become, by a change in the wheel of fortune, the leading group in a cottage.

Closely allied to this is a second need, the *need to be allowed to be different*. Cottages as we know have climates, cultures, even reputations of their own. "All the girls in X cottage do this, or this, or that." How many of you do not have on your campus a cottage that has such and such reputation, never mind how often children or housemother change? Part of this is, of course, healthy. It is group solidarity. But sometimes it means that a child can only buy acceptance in the group by surrendering his individual tastes and even his own sense of right and wrong. Sometimes it is a bloc of children, usually those who have been too long together or too long in that institution; sometimes it is a single leader or even the memory of a leader who cannot let others be different. And here we need to be careful of the child who is assigned a role which looks on the surface different but is really an imposed difference— the scapegoat, the clown, the "cottage idiot" (like the village idiot of old), the licensed "screwball" and even the mascot, the little one whom everyone loves. These are not real differences. They are searching for likeness through difference. A real difference means that the child who likes to read, or to get good grades, or does not like girls, or who likes the unpopular staff member, should be accepted for what he is and not forced to dissemble or kowtow to the prevailing fashion.

A third need is the *need to be able to belong to other groups as well*. It is so easy to make a cottage a completely self-contained unit. Indeed as we moved from mass care to recognizing the importance of belonging to a small group of one's peers, and as houseparents moved from being "matrons" carrying out the boss' orders to being child-care workers responsible for a group of children we ran into the danger of thinking of the cottage as the all-in-all. But this is not the way that we ourselves use groups in our daily life. We belong to one at home, another at work, a third in the church and a fourth, perhaps at play. Since one of the values of group living is the opportunity for many and varied relationships a child needs a chance to belong to different groups on different levels.

I recognize that this is not always as easy as it sounds. It is far easier to do everything as a cottage—to sit as a cottage in church, or at meals, if one should eat centrally, and even to have an invisible wall round the play area of a cottage, so that the houseparent knows what is going on. And of course there are things that a cottage should do together, just as a family does. But one of the reasons that I like the family or mixed cottage is that it helps many children belong to two groups at the same time—his peers or natural companions and his family. It also breaks down cottage walls based on sex or age.

School and church can also offer a chance of an alternative or a supplementary group, but only of course, if the child is really part of the different group. If the child merely attends the school or the church in question, and is whisked away the moment classes or service are ended in a special bus without the chance to participate in the various informal groups that make up school or church life he has no real opportunity to belong to any other group. But even on campus, in work details, in common playgrounds, in clubs, or in projects, some variety can be provided.

This leads me to my fourth need, and a very important one it is. This is the *need to escape sometimes*. No, I do not mean to run away, although sometimes running away is the way in which a child expresses this particular need. It is the need for short periods not to have to be part of a group, and it can be met in a number of different ways. I would in fact suggest four of them. One is by having somewhere where the child can be alone, or possibly with a friend or two, in a bedroom, perhaps, or on the grounds. Some children even in families are forced to find this privacy in the bathroom, which accounts for the fact that this is the most disputed room in the average American home.

Another way is through vacations or even week-ends with family or friends or sponsors. Any of you who has ever had in his home a child from a group-living situation knows that what he wants to do is not to have anything planned for him, to be able to lie around all day and read comics or mooch through the woods; anything rather than be part of a group or be scheduled to do this or that.

A third way is to have sometimes, somewhere an experience of a one-to-one relationship, if only when the child is sick, or every one else goes to the movies, or in a private talk with housemother or superintendent. Talks with the caseworker, too, if they are not, as they all too often are, tied to times of trouble, can offer another kind of escape: escape from the present and the here into the future and what is happening "out there."

A fourth way is to be permitted to hold something back from the group, to have to some extent one's private world. This, of course, can be an unhealthy kind of escape if the child is forced to it through lack of other means of escape, but some of it is natural, and enjoins upon all of us, housemother, caseworker or whom have you, not to demand that a child share everything with us.

A fifth need—and we are back now in our major classification, the intangible needs of group living, is *the need to be appreciated by different people for different things*. One of the most important things that the coach, the maintenance man and the farmer contribute to group living is the fact that they are not bound by the child's official reputation. They do not need to know, or to care even if they know, that Jane is a nuisance in the cottage, or is failing in school, or chattered in church, if there is something in their relationship with the child which they can approve. It has been said that every child deserves at least one indulgent parent, and every child in an institution deserves the chance of being especially liked by someone for factors not connected with his overall progress, if it only be for a smile or a likeness to someone else. I sometimes feel when I have spent three or four days on a campus that what I have said or done officially will perhaps vanish very soon, but that my particular liking for a certain kind of unsatisfactory, rambunctious, rather hostile alley-cat or "raggedy-Ann" may in the long run turn out to be more significant.

The sixth and seventh needs are perhaps rather obvious. They are the *need to possess something of one's own*, one's very own, which is being met more adequately than it was, and the *need to be able to give sometimes*. Children in institutions are so much given to. Everything is provided for them. Their chances to give in return are often very slight. It meant so much to one cottage, when they were taken for a picnic by some kindly organization, to club together and tip the bus-driver. We sometimes forget in our working with children that when we say that it is more blessed to give rather than to receive we do not mean only that those who give will be blessed some time in the future or in another life. We are talking about the here and now. Man has a deep need to give, and although some of our upset children find it difficult indeed, they do need the experience.

And so we come to our eighth and last need—not that we could not find many others, but eight is enough at one time. This is the *need for constructive leadership*. However well a group is constructed, however congenial it is, it needs the leadership of a person concerned about all of its components, the person who comes to the rescue of those who are left out and takes the heat off the oppressed, the person who is both part of the group, able to identify with its essential values, but who sets limits on it and gives it some sense of direction. In other words, the houseparent, who is both parent and group-leader.

But it must be constructive leadership and not control. There is a great difference. I have recently had the experience of working with the houseparents of three cottages of that most difficult age, early adolescence, where the child is facing the prospect of living for the next three or four years in an institution and trying to grow up at the same time. In one the houseparent had control but was offering little leadership. She was keeping the lid on the cottage and she had so far succeeded in avoiding a real clash. But her children were either very cautious and careful and quite lost without her strong hand or were saving up their resentment only to have it result a year or two later in a rejection of the Home and all that went with it. In another a series of houseparents had failed to give leadership enough and the children had developed what might be called an adolescent culture of their own, with values that were quite opposed to those of the Home. In the third a houseparent had been able to be both with her children and an adult at the same time. She was the sort of houseparent who could sympathize with the girls about their boy-friends and appreciate what it meant to be jilted at fifteen, but whose judgment as to what limits to set on these relationships was respected by her girls, because, as one of them expressed it, "Although I can't agree with everything she does and says, in the end I know that she is on our side."

It is, of course, no easy business to achieve true leadership—to know when to be the same as one's children, thinking like them and seeing things through their eyes, and when to be different, to be an adult and if necessary the boss. But the success of group-living depends to no small extent on how skilfully this is done. And I know some houseparents who do a beautiful job of it.

Group living, then, can be most helpful to many children if it is recognized as fulfilling a part only of a child's need, if it is balanced with other needs, and if real attention is paid to the needs of a child to vary it in the kind of way that we have discussed here. Let me enumerate them again, and say again that group living can be, and is, a marvellous instrument of help, provided that it meets the child's need

    to be included if one wants to, but only then,
    to be allowed to be different,
    to belong to other groups as well as to the primary one,
    to escape from the group sometimes,
    to be appreciated by different people for different things,
    to possess something of one's own,
    to be able to give as well as to receive,
and finally, for constructive leadership.

I have no fear in this respect. More and more I see these needs considered and met by children's institutions. But sometimes we need to be sure, to look at ourselves and see if, by any chance, the ever-pressing business of daily life has not caused us to overlook an important need.

6.

Likenesses and Differences in Various Types of Group Care*

THIS QUESTION has often been asked: What is there in common among a church home for dependent children, a state-sponsored detention facility, a school for the deaf or blind, or even a hospital for spastics? Are not the type of children cared for, the purposes of the agency, even the way in which children come to them so different that there is little that they can discuss together and learn, or teach, each other?

On an immediate program level there is some truth in this contention. A discussion on selective intake has little meaning, for instance, for a detention home which must take what the police bring it. Teaching methods for the blind are irrelevant in a home where all the children are sighted. And we do not get very far with the sort of pious pronouncement that children are children wherever they are.

But we may be a little nearer finding a common ground if we think that we are all dealing with children who are away from their own homes, for this has certain implications. It means that we are caring for children who fundamentally do not want to be with us. By this I do not mean that all of them would choose, here and now, to return to their particular homes or that they do not see some advantage in being with us, but that everyone of them in their hearts wish that it had not happened, and every one of them is asking the often unspoken but nevertheless omnipresent question: "What is wrong with me? What have I done, or what am I, that my parents did not love me? That I have fallen foul of the law? That I was born crippled? That I am different from other children?" In this the differences between the dependent and the delinquent, the whole and the crippled, tend to disappear. These are all children whom life in some way has let down, who have lost in some measure the three basic trusts which make life liveable—trust in one's fellows (specifically trust in adults if one happens to be a child), trust in oneself, in one's own worthwhileness, and trust in God or Providence, in the right ordering of the world. And I would say to any facility for the care of children away from home, whatever its purpose,

* Given at the Florida Group Child Care Association Meeting, Orlando, Florida, September 1961.

whatever its sponsorship, that the primary object of its study should be how these three trusts can be restored.

Secondly we are united through the common use, as part but not the whole of our caring, of a particular tool or method, inherent in this paper's title. We all make use, whether we are conscious of it, of that remarkable instrument of child care, the group—that instrument which can offer a child security on the one hand, routine and a predictable life, and yet give him opportunity to remake his relationships, restore his trust in people, at his own speed and with whom, at the moment, he can find it possible to trust; that instrument, on the other hand, for which we have been most criticized when it has been allowed to become not group-care but mass-handling. Whether we are conscious of groups, whether we plan them with care, have reduced them to their most useful size, are concerned with their inter-relationships, see them as one of our greatest assets, or whether we just care for children in groups as a means of dealing with numbers of children or because that is how our buildings are constructed, the group is there, tight or flexible, restrictive or enlarging, at war or at peace with other groupings, harmful or helpful to the child, manageable or out of hand, pro- or anti-administration, and the climate and the productiveness of our cottage or dormitory, even the use that our children can make of school or church or doctor will be greatly affected by it. Thus we have a common interest in what happens to children in groups—in the construction of groups and in their management, in the making of this tool the fine instrument it can be, in being proud to be practitioners of the art of group care.

But more than that. Because we are all dealing with children away from home, because we are all of us, hopefully structured to meet the needs of such children, we need to recognize that these children have three needs. We may not deal with them all equally, and by our very nature we may concentrate on one and think of it as our major service, but nevertheless these needs exist and are often interdependent. Ignoring any one of the three may vitiate the others.

The first is the need for a *living experience* that is rich and productive, that allows for growth and learning in the widest sense. Under this I include all that we think of as program, as education, as care, as love and leadership and discipline, as worship and recreation.

The second is *help in relating to what has happened to one or is happening or indeed likely to happen.* Under this I subsume such questions as, "Why am I here? Where do I go from here? What is my relationship with the life that I have left?" and all that goes into planning for restoration of the family, for living apart from it or for finding a new one. It is the kind of need which the study, *Children in Need of Parents,* found to be so lacking in our child-care programs today. And it is to this need, rather than or perhaps prior to selective intake, or treatment of "problem," that skilled casework ought to speak.

And the third is what I might call *remedial care,* the overcoming of handicap, whether this be physical, or emotional (as in the instance of the so-called "treatment center"), or educational, or a matter of handling a handicap successfully.

Now it seems to me that emphasis or over-emphasis on one of these needs to the exclusion of others has not only sometimes made it hard for agencies to learn from each other, but has crippled the agencies themselves and prevented them from doing as good a job as they should with what they see as their primary service.

Let us take the living experience first. To many agencies the need for a rich living experience is obvious. This is what they exist to give. But others have not been so clear. I know for instance a spastic hospital which has the finest remedial care. But perhaps because it is staffed primarily by doctors, nurses and physiotherapists it has forgotten the need of children for consistent living, for someone to turn to for the little things of life, for leadership and protection—in short for the kind of thing that a houseparent provides. And although this may seem an extreme example, something of the same danger may exist in an institution whose purpose is primarily remedial. It is inherent, for instance, in the original concept of the Training School—a school, not somewhere where one lives—and may account, in some instances, for the kind of congregate living that the child is expected to endure in some Training Schools while he is being re-trained, although recently Training Schools have recognized this problem and have, in some instances, led the way in such matters as the training of houseparents. This same neglect of daily living has, I think, muddied the waters when we begin to talk of institutions becoming "treatment centers" and either deny the treatment that comes from a rich living experience, or, which to me is worse, try to make living "treatment" in the clinical sense, to eliminate from it the spontaneity and warmth, the love and anger and impulsiveness of which living is comprised. Both, maybe under the same eventual direction and with the same purpose in mind, are what helps the child. The spastic will learn his muscle-control and the blind his Braille or his self-management in proportion to the way in which his living needs are met. I teach a lot of blind students, most of them pupils of a State School for the blind, and it is interesting to see how their adequacy reflects not so much their teaching as the quality of life they were able to find in that school.

But there is another factor, and one that should warn us against too great a reliance on living experience alone. All these blind students feel a great loss, and this is not the loss of their eyes alone.

It is the sense of not having parents in quite the same way as others, of being "away at school." Despite the obvious reason for being away from home, doubts arise about their parents' love, about their positions in the home circle. Some were hindered in their learning from homesickness, from the absence of letters or visits. Some were plagued with vague feelings that they or their parents had sinned. Do you remember that this was the first question the apostles asked of Jesus when he healed the man blind from birth—"who did sin, this man or his parents?" Some had been helped, by caseworkers or wise teachers. But how much more does the child who is away from home for less obvious reasons need this kind of help?

In this particular area, the working with the child about his home situation, the working with the whole family towards either rehabilitation, or surrender, or a satisfactory and supporting relationship while the child is away from home, some institutions for dependents have led the way. But other homes for dependents have relied too much on their living experience to cure all ills, and as a result are losing half of what their otherwise excellent programs are giving. I know one home for instance that seems to have everything to give—small cottages, comfort, well-trained staff, excellent education. But it is losing far too many of its children in adolescence, as unmanageable or "no longer able to make use of the Home," and its graduates, although in some ways very estimable people, are characterized by conformity, a shallowness of emotion and the psychosomatic tension diseases such as asthma, ulcers and colitis. It also has an undue proportion of marriages in the first year after graduation. These are children who have never come to terms with life except as a dangerous thing to live fully, who are driven to seek for safety in withdrawal, conformity or dependence.

Children in Need of Parents showed up the plight of the institution for dependents, although I think its answer was the wrong one. Before we cancel out one set of parents and find the child new ones I want to be much surer than we are that we have used every atom of skill in our power to help the old ones. But how much more, I wonder, does not the child in the institution for delinquents need someone to work with him about his parents and to work with his parents, too? For not only is his home the place where his delinquency grew, but he has lost it through his own act of delinquency. More than any other child he feels unloved and he feels it to be his fault that he is so. The failure to work with the family of the delinquent boy or girl until the child returns to them seems to me one of the greatest weaknesses in our program for such children today. We seem to assume in this field that the child can somehow be disentangled from his hates and loves towards those very people whom he first learned to love and hate and we find out, only too often, that this is not so. Even our laws all too often support us in this. The parents of a delinquent child are almost forcibly made irresponsible. They are relieved of all financial duty while the child is away from home; his very coming back into the community where he is now expected to behave is often the cause of added burdens to the family. And even in hospitals today we know that contact with the parents may be the difference between getting well and staying sick.

It is in the third element, the type of remedial care we give, that most of our differences lie. We differ not only in the nature of this remedial care, but in the emphasis that we put on it. Some of us may feel little need for remedial program—perhaps only some special schooling or minor medical correction—and others must give prominence to it, since it is the reason for which they exist. But let us be careful neither to ignore it completely nor to make of it the only thing we do. The child's other needs must be met, and too much insistence on any one of the three is self-defeating.

We differ also on procedure, but this is perhaps less important than we sometimes believe. It is true that at the moment a discussion of intake policy may seem academic to a state training school where children are committed by a court without the institution's say-so, but a sound understanding of what children can use group-care and who cannot may become important as an educational tool. It may be at the moment frustrating to talk about cottage grouping to an institution which has a congregate facility, but institutions change and change because of ideas that they have found in others. And there are many things that we can contribute to each other. I was surprised this year at the Chapel Hill Workshops to find in my group entitled, "How can we help our children find a firmer faith in God?" that the participant who contributed more genuine understanding of children's problems in accepting God as Father came not from a church institution, but from a State Training School, and to hear him say afterwards that in his seven years of attendance he had never found a workship so useful in a down-to-earth practical way.

There is a large common core. We all need to be interested in groups and grouping, in the training of houseparents, in certain aspects of program—and perhaps the newest kind of institution, the Boy's Ranch or Children's Village has something to tell us here, especially about self-government—in the kind of buildings we need, in parents, and the ways we can use to help them be more responsible for their children, in buildings and how they can be used, in the nature and extent of community participation, in the problems of the early adolescent who faces a long period of living away from home and yet wants to be independent, in boy-girl relationships (particularly maybe if we have only boys or girls in our institution), in creating in our agencies a real sense of the team, in job description and personnel practices, in what we do ourselves and what we delegate to others, in a better understanding of discipline and what it means to a child, in the whole quality of living and understanding that we provide.

But there is a kind of difference that I hope that we will maintain, and which seems to me more important than the kind of inevitable difference that we have discussed today. This is the difference that comes from being an individual, both as a person and an agency. It is really the freedom to be different, to try new ideas or stick to the old ones, if they seem good to us, and not because of some theory or fashion in welfare. This also means the freedom to go on being stupid or cruel or unimaginative, and states, it seems to me, ought to be able to put some limits on that. For the genius of this field, and the reason I think that it has grown so remarkably in quality in the last ten or twenty years, is that there are not any blueprints, that people have dared to be different, that more and more institutions are finding out what they want to do and experimenting with it, that there is such difference in the field.

The institutional field is one that is only beginning to find itself. There are a vast number of things about all the subjects I have mentioned as our common core of concern that, thank goodness, we do not know and that we will have to test out bit by bit. The same is true about the whole helping process. And so let us be proud of being different, let us build on what we have, our traditions, our convictions, our observation, and let us resolutely keep our experts on tap but not on top.

7.

The Training and Recruitment of Houseparents*

THERE MAY BE some of you who expect me, from the title assigned to me, to tell you of some hidden reservoir of houseparent material, hitherto untapped, or some magic way of enticing people into the work, or some philosopher's stone by which the poor houseparent may be transmuted into gold. These will be disappointed. There have been a few experiments, such as the use of seminary student wives and their husbands or appeals to those on Social Security to fill houseparent ranks, but nothing like a simple answer, and, indeed the usual sources, the retired, the widow, and the occasional church worker who feels a call to this particular work remain our chief and not always satisfactory sources of supply. Indeed with the use of community schools and better conditions in public teaching one useful source in the past has begun to dry up on us, and the houseparent of 1961 is not essentially different in education, marital status, previous experience working with people, length of service, and I might say in "real wages" than she was fifteen years ago. She is still, or still was three years ago, on an average 53 years of age, as likely as not to be a widow, a high school but not a college graduate, and to have been on her job somewhere between three and four years.

Yet one of the most remarkable things in the whole history of child care has been the way in which the houseparent has changed. What used to be, with some notable exceptions, a timid, dependent group, hesitant in expressing opinion, rigid and insensitive in most of their ideas, unwilling to face realistically the deep emotional problems of their children or even the natural course of their development—the group for whom I once coined the unkind phrase of "decayed Christians"—has become an eager, self-confident group of semi-professionals, some of whom show remarkable skills.

How has this miracle come about? Some of it may be due to wise selection on your part, to an insistence that where there is choice

* Given to the Presbyterian Association of Children's Homes, Anchorage, Kentucky, April 1961.

you plump for the mature hitherto successful person rather than the good lady who needs charity herself. But often you have little choice. You have to take what the Lord provides. Some of it is due, in those institutions where this has happened, to much smaller groups and more community contacts But chiefly it has been due to what you have done to train and develop your houseparent staff.

This country has been thought of as somewhat laggard in houseparent training. In England and Belgium, for instance, where public rather than private Homes are the rule, a certified houseparent has a year of professional training at government expense. Some efforts of this kind have been tried in this country. But I think we need to be very careful before we put our trust wholly in what the houseparent knows. The least of the problems in teaching or training people in the helping professions is what one teaches them. It is how one helps them want to learn and how one helps them put not only what they know but what they are into practice. Proficiency in the job is so largely a matter of what one thinks about one's job, what it expects of one, the kind of support one gets in it, and in the last analysis what discipline one is willing to acquire to become proficient in it.

The beginning, in fact, of houseparent training takes place when the houseparent stops being a "matron" and becomes a houseparent. It will advance further when she genuinely becomes a child-care worker. It moved forward when, for the first time in this country, a publisher thought it worth while to publish a book of readings for houseparents and a guide for child-care workers. It continues whenever you send a houseparent to a conference, and whenever this conference stops being a series of lectures by experts and becomes a forum where houseparents can say their piece and have their ideas valued; when in fact they can speak as well as be spoken to. It happens whenever you invite what teen-agers call a "professor-type professor" to your campus to work with houseparents and he is interested in what they do and how they do it. It happens when you begin to see administration not as hierarchy in which the houseparent carries out your commands, but as a help to the worker who lives with the child both day and night, when the houseparent is truly a member of the team with as much in her sphere to contribute as the professional in his. It happens when the administrator or director of cottage life schedules regular conferences with the houseparent, thereby treating her as a professional, and does not see her only when things are going wrong; when he evaluates her performance objectively and in accordance with standards, and entrusts her with information that she needs to carry out her job. It does not depreciate modern psychology or the theory of groups, or any other sphere of knowledge important to the job to say that more important than this knowledge itself is the fact that you want her to have it.

But this is not the whole story. Houseparent training becomes a reality when the houseparent knows what is expected of her and what to expect in her job, and when she is freed from the need to protect herself at every turn. For only in this security can she develop professional discipline.

As I look back on the more than a thousand houseparents I have known and worked with—some, it is true, narrow and apparently insensitive to children's needs, some just plainly inefficient, but many with much to give to children and a few truly professional people—I am inclined to say that what characterizes the good ones has been a freedom from fear, internal and external. It is not, of course, the whole story, but it is a big bit of it.

These are the ones who know what their job is and are clear about their role. They do not have to feel wholly responsible or to hug their children to themselves. Both professionally and personally they are able to share with others. They have neither the fear of not being loved nor the fear of losing control.

They are the ones who know the rules and yet are not afraid to break them if the need arises. The most helpful single thing I have seen a houseparent do was a breach of the institution rules—the inviting of a parent to cook a dinner in a cottage whereby for the first time in his life—he was a skilled cook—he had the experience of shining before his daughter and she could be proud of him and herself. They are those who do not panic at the ups and downs of relationships or think that they will be criticized because at the moment their cottage is in a "down." They are those who know that the best housemother is not always the most popular and who can risk themselves in relationship, knowing that they will not be held responsible if a child makes the wrong choice. They are those who do not have to nag—and the nagging houseparent is the one whom children resent the most—but are not afraid to be firm.

I have just been working with one of these. She is facing what seems to me one of the biggest challenges that housemothers and indeed institutions face today. This is the time of decision that the long-time dependent child goes through at from fourteen to sixteen before he makes up his mind, if he does so, to remain in our care. We are, some of us, justly proud of our product, our graduate, but we lose far too many children who become unmanageable in their early or middle teens. Sometimes what happens is that these children, choosing to rely more on themselves than on adult guidance, develop what might be called an adolescent sub-culture whose values are very different from ours. Some come through and settle down.

Too many—and even a few is too many—do not and become hostile to us or do things that we cannot sanction.

The more we look at such sub-cultures, in institutions or in their more serious manifestation as the "delinquent city gang"—and the two phenomena are not as different as we might hope—the more we know that to work with them needs first and foremost an ability to approve what is good in them as well as to set limits on them. This cannot be done if the housemother is afraid that holding hands inevitably leads to kissing and kissing to less desirable practices, or if she is constantly afraid of what other houseparents or the administration thinks of her children or her cottage. It needs, to put it in its real content, a deep understanding of an essential Christian truth, which is that we live no longer under a Covenant of Law, with its fearful and meticulous safeguards against doing anything which might incline us to sin, but under a Covenant of Grace, in which sin is seen primarily as the selfish or prideful use of the good gifts which God has given us.

The fearful person cannot be understanding. The housemother who tries to solve her boy-girl relationships by strewing broken glass under the bushes succeeds far less than the one who can laugh with a girl about her boy-friend but who stands four-square for a wise use of the relationship and who knows where to draw the line.

While we are talking theologically, let us look for one minute at the religious houseparent. There have been many lists drawn up of the qualities of the ideal houseparent. She is patient, understanding, loving, firm, mature, flexible and "able to take it." She has a sense of humor and a wide lap and an ability to be firm where necessary. But few seem to include statements about the quality of her religious life, and this is surely of primary importance, if it relates to the "quality" and not the "quantity" of her religion.

The interesting thing about the religious houseparent is that there are always two sides to her religion. On the one side is narrow moralism, a carefulness and a tendency to judge adversely. On the other there is an amazing tolerance, a willingness to understand, a deep feeling of common humanity and a Christian humility which is of the stuff of which great housemothers are made. And in most cases these two, the negative and the positive reflections of religion, exist at one and the same time and in the same person. The love, the forgiveness and even the flexibility is there but houseparents are afraid to use it. They doubt their own ability, or are afraid that they are not supposed to use it, or that they will be blamed if anything in the least questionable happens. Sometimes I think they are not sure how much you want them really to love.

And so I am going to say something which may seem to you very hard. I do not of course mean it absolutely. There are some people who cannot change, who are sick or inadequate or so damaged by life that they cannot be helped to be free. They cannot learn. But by and large you will get the kind of service from your houseparents that you yourself deserve. If you really want them to learn, most of them will; if you can free them from fear, they will blossom; if your philosophy is one of service and love, they will be able to use their gifts in the same way. If you trust them, they will trust children and children will trust them in return. If you are fearful, in your heart, whatever you may say on the surface, they will be fearful, too. If you love them and individualize them, they will have a greater chance to love and individualize children.

There is much yet to explore in what helping houseparents means and in attracting better material. There is the whole question of the younger houseparent, the one who makes it her career. In some situations she may be valuable but I would not give up on the grand-mother. She has a role yet to play. There is the very important question of finding more men as houseparents and their use in the institution and some of you may know my contention that the group that needs them most is the little girls. But what we have done is not so bad, and, constantly on my travels, I stand in awe of the potential I see, sometimes buried but still apparent, in some of these people to give of themselves to children.

8.

The Place of the Staff Member Who Is Not a Houseparent*

A CHILDREN'S HOME is a place where a child learns to trust again. Let down by his family, fearful that his own unlovableness has been the cause of family breakdown, unable to understand the misfortune that has come to him, the child entering the children's home today has lost faith in his parents, in himself, and in the God who has ordained such a trial for him.

This trust the Home sets out to foster both through the way the child lives in the Home and through its work with his parents. While at the bottom of all help is understanding—understanding of why the child may be resentful of those who replace his natural parents, or why he may cling to inadequate parents, or why he may become indifferent, wasteful of the things he is given, or fearful of making normal relationships—the Home in its very structure has certain things which are helpful.

A Home is a place where one lives in groups. That is its first characteristic and where it differs from other methods of child care, such as the foster family home. The group helps him share his problem and takes the edge off his isolation. A Home is also a place where there are certain routines and schedules. Wisely used these are helpful to the mistrustful child. They assure him that life is stable and secure.

But a Home is not merely a place of safety. It is a place where a child can re-learn a trust in people—and hence in turn trust in himself and in God—at his own pace and step by step. Often the person whom he finds hardest to trust at first is his housemother. She is the one taking the place of the mother he cannot give up. She is the one who has to discipline him most of the time. In the end we want him to relate positively to her, but this may have to be a gradual process.

This is where the "outside" worker comes in—the cook, the handyman, the painter, the work supervisor, the laundry worker, the pastor, the farmer. It is to these people that a child may move first. They have two great advantages over the housemother—they are not taking the mother's place and they do not have to know all of the child's many transgressions—that he was noisy in the dining

* Given to the Staff of Buckner Orphan Home, Dallas, Texas, June 1960.

room or failed to make his bed this morning. They may be the steps in the ladder which help the child regain his trust.

I wish I could tell you all the times I have seen a boy or a girl helped tremendously through his relationship with one of these outside workers. But I think I will tell you of three. One was a boy of low I.Q., overgrown, unambitious, moody and sullen in the cottage, about whom everybody was concerned and somewhat hopeless, but who nevertheless obviously began to change, to become more content and at ease with himself. Why, we could not see until in the chorus of disapproval the farmer spoke up, "That boy is the best durn manure-spreader I've ever had on the place." He then turned on the staff meeting and told them, "What's wrong with the place is that it's trying to make Persians out of its alley-cats. Why, can't it be content to make its alley-cats better ratters?" This boy had found in the farmer someone who accepted him for what he was —a good alley-cat—and through this was beginning to restore his faith in mankind.

The second was an eleven year old girl who told me, deeply troubled, how she could not be sure who loved her and who did not because, as it seemed to her, as soon as she tried to love someone that someone took advantage of her or pushed her away. I suspect that her way of showing love was somewhat clumsy and uncouth. But when I asked her if there was not something she could trust she said she thought there was something. One could always trust the church. Her face lit up—"and the preacher, too. I feel safe with him." We later detailed the preacher to give her special attention for a while.

The third was a boy of fourteen who had been sick for a long time, was undersized and had lost confidence in his own manhood. The other boys scorned him. Even his housemother, with fifteen other boys to care for, was apt to treat him as the ten-year-old he seemed to be. It was the handyman who recognized his need to be a man and gave him a sense of power again in running the motor mower.

That is why it is the responsibility of each and every employee of a Children's Home to be or do three things:

(1) to be good at their jobs—a good farmer, a good cook

(2) to teach their skill with understanding, and

(3) to take a special interest in the children working for them; to be available when and where the child needs them.

Men have a special responsibility on a campus such as this where father-people are few. They have responsibility to be the kind of men that little boys can admire and look up to. That is generally understood. What is not so often appreciated is what it means to fatherless little girls—and some not so little—to have a man admire them and value them for being little girls. It is something every little girl needs to help her come to terms with the world's requirement that she give up being a tomboy and become a lady. There should be a requirement that no man pass a little girl on the campus without at least a "hello, sweetheart," and a smile.

There are, of course, ways in which the special kind of relationship which an "outside" worker has with a child can be harmful and not helpful. There is, for instance, the "outside" worker who interprets the child's confidence as something the worker himself has created, who begins to say to himself, "John likes me and not his housemother; therefore the housemother is wrong." There is the worker who takes sides with the child against the housemother, the Dean, the Superintendent, and in fact all the rest of the Home. Such a worker does not understand that the child's move to him is natural, part of the learning-to-trust process, and not personal at all. Such a worker is indulging his own need to be loved rather than working to help the child. He is not a member of the team.

But there is, on the other hand, the worker who fails to make use of his special position, who feels it is his duty to correct the child all the time, who will not listen to his problems or let him express his feelings at all. I have heard it said on the campus that one cannot let a child criticize the Home or another staff-member. One certainly cannot if one means by this letting him draw one in in his battle with Home, or Dean, or Houseparent. But children do need someone to talk with safely about their feelings and some understanding that although you feel with him you respect the other staff-member too. This often helps him come to terms with that other worker. A team is not a collection of people each going their own way, heedless of the coach's strategy. But also it is not a collection of people all doing exactly the same thing. Everyone does his specialized part.

For a Home really to help a child it needs the skills of each one of you. It needs a pooling of all your knowledge about each and every child. But it needs first of all a staff who are not jealous of each other, or defensive because Jane at the moment relates to you and not to me, who can understand children's love and resentment and do not take it personally, who can come together to discuss children without being defensive and who are united in their selfless dedication to serving the children with whom they all work.

9.

How Much of a Parent Can I Be?*

THERE HAVE BEEN, as I see it, three stages in the way in which institutions have looked on the parents of children. Their first impulse was to ignore them; to discourage them, if you like, to consider their work well done if the institution could replace the parent both physically and psychologically. These ideas, let us say, came from a positive feeling on our part—our protective feeling for children. But this protectiveness proved inadequate. Only a very few institutions are still at this stage in their thinking.

Then, those who worked with children began to realize that parents were—what shall I say—necessary evils in a child's life. That is, they were frequently a nuisance to the institution, but if the child was to grow normally—and sometimes if he was to be able to accept institutional life at all—his parents had to be taken into account. This led to a good deal of encouragement of parents, both for practical and for idealistic reasons. It led even to the welcoming of parents and to their use by the institution for the child's good. Many institutions today have arrived at this point and many are untiring in a most praiseworthy effort to preserve family ties.

But this philosophy is not, it seems to me, enough. Parents are not simply useful if somewhat capricious aids to institutional adjustment or to normal growth. There is developing in this country the beginnings, at least, of an understanding that the placement of a child may be more than a matter of providing a child with a substitute, or even a better way of life. Placement can be a process that can help a dying family take a new lease on life. It can be an experience through which the whole family grows and gets back on its feet.

It can be, I say. It often is not. Let me say something about the conditions under which this growth can or cannot take place.

A parent has, for some reason, been unable to fulfill his complete

* Given to the Florida Group Child Care Association, Tampa, Florida, September 1956, and revised for publication in *Readings for Houseparents in Children's Institutions,* edited by Alan Keith-Lucas and A. M. Broten (Chicago: Werkman's Book House, 1958). It has been further revised.

parental role. Something has gone wrong in his relationship to the child or in his relationship to life itself. He asks, or the Court requires, that he give up for the time being a very important part of his parental responsibility—the physical care of his child, its training, instruction, and discipline.

Now this can be the occasion for the parent to divest himself of all responsibility. After all, what he has been through has been both an unpleasant and a discouraging experience. He may feel too that having lost, apparently indefinitely, the most obvious part of his parenthood—the physical care of his child—the little bit he has left to him is not worth the keeping. It is not pleasant to visit one's child and realize what one has lost. It is not pleasant to face the fact that someone else is doing a better job with him. It is not pleasant to be *allowed,* or even encouraged by a nice kindly institution, to visit or to write letters. I think that many parents have felt this way and have, as a result, drifted out of their children's lives in a cloud of frustration, pique, and discouragement. Or they have fought the situation, blindly but effectively, with unkept promises, appeals to the child's loyalty, so that the child is forever living in one place and trying to live in another.

But being relieved of the necessity of providing physical care can work in another way. It can be a challenge to a parent—both a challenge and a crutch. It can be an opportunity to learn to be a parent again by trying one's muscles, as it were, on the limited bits of responsibility that do fall to a parent in an institution, free from the overwhelming problems of full parenthood. Just as one who has broken a leg learns by taking little, restricted steps again, so a parent who is not strong enough for the whole job can learn again what it means to be a parent through visiting, through providing financial support, through being consulted about his child's welfare, through providing vacations, while his child is away from home.

He can only do so, however, only under certain conditions, of which the most important seem to me the following:

First, that he have a definite status, a definite and understood set of responsibilities and rights while his child is under care. This moreover should be arrived at either by agreement or as a matter of law. It cannot be something given him out of the institution's bounty. That is why the U.S. Children's Bureau recommends the use of definite terms to indicate the responsibilities that a parent gives up and retains when his child is placed. The bureau calls these responsibilities "legal custody" and "guardianship of the person," the first of which goes to the institution, the second of which the parent keeps. The terms are, I think, open to question since lawyers have their own frequently divergent ways of defining these two powers, and sometimes even use them interchangeably. What is important, it seems to me, is the clear recognition that the parent who has lost physical possession of his child is still entitled to rights and, perhaps more important, is still held responsible for his further actions.

Along with this must go, however, the agency's help. This help consists among other things of keeping the parent clear and aware of how he stands—what he can do and how he can do it. It means helping him make use of the institution's policy. It involves, of course, helping him with his feelings about the whole experience. It includes encouraging him when he shows signs of becoming responsible and being tough with him when he will not.

Being tough does not mean taking harsh or punitive action. It means helping the parent be aware of what his defection is doing to his child and how it may make it impossible for the institution to help the child all it could. It means not letting things rock along year after year with a minimal sort of contact between parent and child.

This, I think, is the chief danger of halfway believing in parents, that we should indulge them by letting them believe that a minimal sort of contact—a letter three times a year, an unkept promise to visit, a token financial payment—is better than nothing at all. It is not. If that is all a parent is willing to do, then he ought to be helped to realize that what he is doing is insufficient—that he is shirking his basic job. The institution must ask him, with all the help that it can give him, to choose between accepting his responsibility or deciding to give it up. It must be ready to bring the matter up for decisions in the courts, if necessary not on the ground that the mother or father is inadequate, depraved, or unworthy to care for his children (which he is not in any case doing) or that our study of his past actions shows him to be rejecting or immature, but that he has decided not to fulfill a responsibility which the law has placed on him. For this is, in the last analysis, and except as we are dealing with the mentally very sick, a matter of decision. More and more, as I have worked in this field, I have been impressed with how similar are the cases which come to us by voluntary placement and those in which the court has had a hand. I am even going to suggest that the majority of parents who lose custody of their children by court order, after good work by a protective agency, do so in accordance with their own inexpressible, but nevertheless heartfelt, wish for which, however, they cannot take responsibility. They may struggle against their wish and be angry that it is granted, but the wish is there all the same. If you want to test this out, try telling a parent—and meaning it—that if he cannot become more responsible he will have to take his child back.

On the other hand, the decision to give up cannot fairly be made unless the parent has something concrete to give up and until he has been helped to look at the situation in all its ramifications. That is why I have some reservations about the laws that are currently being introduced in many states to make it possible to terminate parental rights if a parent fails to maintain contact with a child in placement. The laws could be of great use, but only, it seems to me, if they are used as a supplement to something like the division of parental powers that I have suggested and only if the parent has had the opportunity to try out the experience of being a partial parent with adequate help from the placement agency. Anything else smacks of depriving a parent of rights that he never knew he had or of punishing him for our neglect of his part in the process. Until we make it truly possible for a parent to have some pride in what he can do for his child in the institution, we cannot blame him if he falls down on the job. And this is impossible if we start by believing him a bad parent, by analysing his past performance under stresses and strains that we can hardly imagine. I believe very strongly in the possibility of redemption when there is help available. I have been fooled too often ever to want to choose for another what his choice should be. We do not let a sick man die without medical help because "he ought to get well" without our help. We ought not to do the same to a family.

The parent's decision may be not to maintain ties but to build them anew with another family and a new community, through adoption. Foster family care, short of legal adoption, in this case is only a shadow of the real tie of belonging that alone can justify the breaking of all familial ties. Adoption, however, involves the parent yielding his last, his ultimate powers. This decision not to be responsible may in fact be the most responsible one that a parent can make. It can, and will, if the parent is helped really to think things through, be made from love, from a desire to give the child what he needs, rather than from lack of love or indifference. And it may be expressed by either legal surrender or, where this too painful, by abandonment. Courts have in general been cautious in acting on abandonment unless there is clear evidence of intent on the parent's part to divest himself forever of his responsibility. I think that this is wise. To make a complete break with the past, to build entirely anew, is to assume in some measure a Divine prerogative which cannot be accepted because we merely *think* it would be good for a child or because we are entitled by the laws of men to sit in judgment on the parents. It must be something, the need for which is, as far as human wisdom can go, incontrovertible. Yet if wisely decided on, wisely planned and wisely interpreted, it can offer a child more than any other service that we are empowered to give. It will never, however, be easy for the child or for the parent.

At the same time I want to make clear that I do not believe that long-time care in an institution is always bad. It can become something not unlike boarding school care if the child has outside ties which mean something to him. Some parents and some relatives can be more of a parent to a child in group care than they could on the outside and need to be that kind of parent. Our Southern institutions are more than places to get into and out of quickly. But the institution cannot do the job alone.

Adoption, then, for the parent who makes this ultimate decision. Return home for those who can manage it. Real support in the institution for those who can give it. But, above all and before all, the opportunity for a parent to discover what being a parent means, to ask himself in the face of what is happening to his family and himself, and with all the help we can give him, "How much of a parent can I be?"

10.

The Nature of the Helping Process*

TO HELP ANOTHER human being may sound like a very simple process. Actually it is one of the hardest things that anyone can be called on to do.

We all know our failures in the field. We know the person who refuses to be helped—the client who won't get medical care, the fellow who won't take the job we offer him, even though it would seem that to do so was the most obvious common sense. We know also the man who accepts our help but uses it in a way that troubles us or seems self-defeating—the public assistance recipient who uses his grant to become more dependent instead of less so, the man who seems to accept our advice but somehow manages to pervert it so that it does him more harm than good. And we know perhaps only too well the person who uses our help as long as we are there to watch over him or "jack him up" but backslides as soon as our back is turned.

Our natural reaction is to blame people who do this to us, or to attribute their failure to get and use help to some inadequacy in them. We label them as immature, or sinful, or uncooperative, or stubborn, or just plain "no 'count." Notice how even in listing here what went wrong with the helping process I have said, "The person or the man who . . ." as if there was something wrong with him.

What do we do then, once we recognize this wrongness? We can do any number of things, and from the Early Church Fathers to the heyday of the Poor Laws and even into the era of modern scientific methods of helping we, and society as a whole, have done one or all of them.

We have sometimes refused to help those who refused to help themselves, or used our help unwisely. We have washed our hands of them. Or, we have tried to force them to do something about themselves by punishing them in some way, through starvation, or shame, or the workhouse, by the whip, or the stocks, or by what is

* First given to representatives of a number of helping professions under the auspices of the Mental Health Associations of South Carolina, Florence, S.C., February 1959. Published in the *Christian Scholar*, Summer, 1960.

known as less-eligibility—the forcing them to live at a level below
what health and decency demands. Or, if we are very patient and
full of a desire to help, we have tried one of three methods, according
to our knowledge and taste. Sometimes we have gone on trying to
help in the same way, believing that in the end the water will wear
away the stone. We have exhorted and urged and persuaded and
bombarded with good advice. Sometimes we have hoped that if
only they could learn to like and admire us, some change might be
forthcoming, and we have been extra nice and non-judgmental and
friendly. And sometimes we have tried to figure out what was wrong
and put it right for such people. We have manipulated their environment, or fixed their teeth, or persuaded their relatives to treat them
more kindly, or judiciously parcelled praise or encouragement, or
tried to get them to see how their feelings have led them astray.

I am not saying that people have not been helped in perhaps all
of these ways. But I do suggest that all of these answers fail to take
into account one very important fact about the helping process—a
fact that may help many people whom we have classified as un-
helpable, and help many of them perhaps on a deeper level than
before.

This is simply the fact that helping is a two-way process, involving
two people, and that what goes wrong in the helping may lie to no
small extent with the person who offers help, or with the process
through which help is being extended.

I cannot pretend that we know all about this process, or that what
we know involves any startling new discoveries. Indeed many of its
principles have been known to man since at least the dawn of the
Christian era. But I do think that the growth of organized helping
has enabled us to look more carefully than perhaps ever before at
what goes on between helper and helped.

To give help really means *to offer someone an opportunity to
change.* All other help is simply a patching up until the next breakdown, necessary perhaps for the moment, but of no lasting significance. This was recognized by such pioneers as the Christian Social-
ists and the Charity Organization leaders of the last century when
they fought to replace casual charity with planned concern for those
in need. But yet these sincere people made one very great mistake.
They thought that what went wrong with the helping that they saw
all around them lay in what was given, and not in how it was given.
They thought that money, or material things, did not offer a frame-
work in which change could take place and that intangible things such
as advice, persuasion and friendly interest did. This is a mistake
still made by many modern helpers, who exalt "services" such as
counselling and ignore the help that can come from something as
prosaic as a public assistance grant.

What these people do not see is that all help is potentially good if the recipient can choose to make use of it, and that no help is good if the recipient does not. So that helping comes to mean *something, tangible or intangible, offered in such a way that the person to whom it is offered can choose to use it*—that is, *choose to change* through its use.

But we do have to be very careful about this word "choose", for we are using it in a rather special sense. To choose to use help means much more than to select a course of action, or even to make up one's mind to do something. It means the decision of the whole person to go along with something, to do something about something, to risk oneself and everything one has in order to get something better. The nearest word to it in our language is the meaning that the church gives to the word "commitment." Man does not "select" God or the Devil. One either commits oneself to God or one doesn't.

It is necessary to understand this special use of the word because the central idea here has only too often been misinterpreted by the practitioners of "permissive" or "non-directive" techniques. This kind of choosing does not mean that the person being helped is free to do anything he wants without suffering the natural consequences, a misunderstanding that has given social workers and ministers and progressive teachers the reputation of being soft-hearted or starry-eyed or unrealistic. It has, as a matter of fact, nothing to do with material freedom or freedom of choice in the usual sense. It can be exercised just as well by a prisoner in a jail as by a public assistance recipient on an inadequate grant or a company executive at his desk. Material restrictions may complicate but can never take away the necessity of this kind of choice.

Still less can this kind of choice be thought of as easy, or made possible by reasoning, or arguing, or exhorting, or persuading, as I know that many ministers know in relation to the kind of commitment with which they are most concerned. One cannot make it because one ought to, or sees good reason for doing so, or because someone else wants one to. For this kind of choice is terribly hard. It is terribly personal. And it is terribly dangerous. Truly, as in a wider context, one must lose one's life to gain it and to ask someone to change is to ask one knows not what.

For making this kind of choice always means at least four things. It means admitting your own failure. It means putting oneself more or less in the power of another, letting him know you and take a part in your life. It means hard work, for the choice has to be made again and again in different contexts, although the fact of having once made it makes it more possible the second and the hundredth time. It means risking the unknown; giving up a present certainty, even though this may be an uncomfortable one, for a good which cannot as yet be fully seen.

The correspondences between the process of asking for human help and the religious experience of conversion are so remarkable that they cannot, I feel, be entirely accidental. The words, repentance, submission, steadfastness under temptation, and faith, are plainly corollary to the four elements that I have described here—a fact that I did not realize until I had set these down with no thought of this parallelism.

I do not suggest that this is the same process. In fact there is one very important difference. The person approaching God for help must submit entirely to His Will. What individuality he maintains is then God's gift. He must also intend his submission to be permanent. The person seeking human help cannot submit to the will of the helper. If he does so defeats his ends. In fact, he must always maintain his integrity as a separate person, against the will of the helper. This is, I would suggest, because the helper's will is of the same imperfect nature as his own and because human will tends to control and not to set free. And again the helped person makes this submission not forever, or even wholly for a time, but for a specific purpose and for a limited length of time. Nevertheless, he must admit the helper to some extent into his life.

I would very tentatively suggest that what we have here is a natural mirror or representation of a divine process and that it should not surprise us. It seems to me entirely proper that there should be such "repetitions of the pattern" at different levels in a consistent universe, and I am given some courage to suggest this by works such as Dorothy Sayers' *The Mind of the Maker,* in which she examines the process of artistic creation as a representation of the Trinity.

If this is what being helped means, is it surprising then that people will do almost anything to prevent themselves from being helped? Is it surprising that many of them refuse to admit their real need? Is it surprising that others demand help of us on their own terms— "give me my check and leave me alone"—as a means of warding off any demand really to change? The demanding client is not simply covering up his embarrassment at asking for help, as he has so often been represented. He is actively fighting his need for help. So is the person who submits to the will of the helping person all the external, unimportant decisions, who indeed thrusts them upon him and becomes what we call dependent, while he "goes through the motions" and remains at the same time unchanged. And so, often enough, is the person who says that he wants help, who does what seems all he can to get it, and yet finds it beyond his grasp.

Let me try to illustrate this with a case. Here, for instance, is a longshoreman with a hernia that can be repaired so that he can do light work. A vocational rehabilitation counsellor helps him get it repaired and finds him a job as a clerk. The client is cooperative. He keeps appointments. He tries to learn what he needs for his new job. He takes a position offered to him. But in a month or two he develops a psychosomatic asthma and has to go to bed again.

He was not a malingerer. The asthma was very real. He did not sit down and figure out: if I get asthma I won't have to work. But in the recesses of his mind he was full of fears. He was afraid of his new job—could he succeed at it? He feared having once more to compete in a world of well men that would make no excuse for him, for he was no longer ill. And maybe he feared too what this new job meant to him. He was no longer the masculine figure tossing bales. He was pushing a pen—an old man's job, a weakling's job, a job that could be done by a girl. And so his mind and his body together threw up a protection for him. If he were sick he was safe from his fears. And this, we are beginning to understand, is the real meaning of much of the sickness, both mental and physical, that we see in this world. More and more diseases are shown to be protections against pressures one cannot stand.

We could say many things about this man and his situation. First, that the pressures were great. Secondly, that "he"—the whole of him, that is—could not make the great decision to get well. His conscious mind could, but not body-and-mind together. He was, in fact, caught between two contradictory forces, his desire to get well and his fear of doing so.

This is a state which, in my profession's peculiar jargon, we call ambivalence—wanting two contradictory things, feeling two ways at once. It is a paralyzing condition, so paralyzing in fact that it often looks like laziness, lack of moral stamina, being content with poor conditions, even feeblemindedness. It is what is "wrong" with so many people that we think are inadequate. And helping becomes then, very often, *making it possible for people to resolve their ambivalence;* helping them choose (in our sense of the word) to get well or not to get well, to change or not to change, to use help or not to use it. And we might say about our longshoreman one more thing: perhaps the helper did not help this man with his ambivalence. Perhaps he ignored it or did not want to believe that it was there.

For there are certain conditions which we know make the resolution of ambivalence more possible and free people to make the kind of choice of which they are capable. And the first, and perhaps the basic one on which all the others depend, is in itself a paradox. It is that *a positive choice is only possible where the opposite choice is also possible and acceptable.*

Intellectually this may not be too hard to see. Man cannot

choose to be good unless he can also choose to be bad. If God had compelled man to be good he would not be good at all. Again, man cannot choose to live fully unless he can also choose (or accept) death. Nothing is gained without risk and to say "Yes" sincerely always means that I could have said "No." We even recognize this when we speak slightingly of the "Yes-man."

But this truth is terribly hard to recognize in practice. We so much want the man we are helping to make the *right* decision, to choose independence and not dependence, God and not the Devil. Even to recognize the possibility that he may choose the wrong seems like treason to us. We work for an agency whose whole purpose is to rehabilitate. How can we freely tell a man that he is free to remain ill?

And yet he cannot choose to get well unless he can choose to be ill. He cannot be pushed or forced or even gently manipulated (one of the strongest forces I know of) into choosing to get well—not if we want a real decision. This is the mistake that so many of us make time and time again—churches, courts, protective agencies, and schools.

Perhaps I can make the point clearer by exporing a little further what is meant here by the opposite, or negative choice. By this I do not mean merely a failure to choose the good (or the supposed good). That is what happens when we try to *make* someone into something that he has not chosen to be, and he fails to live up to expectations. It is utterly defeating. But there is always a negative choice—even a kind of failure—that in itself is a choice and that has something of triumph about it. It is the choice, the determination, not to do what is expected of one, not to have anything to do with this kind of help. It is the decision to "go it alone" or "to take the consequences." And being free to make this choice does not and cannot ever mean being spared these consequences. It is this that man, if he is to be helped, must always be free to do—even to "curse God and die." And we, and even our cherished values, are not, of course, God. What we think of as the wrong choice may for another person be right. Even if it cannot be, the choice must still be there. The risk must be taken. And the person who makes the wrong choice is much closer to help than he who makes no choice at all.

That is why I insisted that help must be help to choose to be well or to choose *not* to be well. All we can do as helping people is to set up those conditions that free a man to make this choice. And thus we come to the second condition, which is a corollary of the first. *The choice must be made by the person helped. It cannot be made, it cannot even be too passionately wished by the helper.* For the helper to put his own will into it takes it away from the will of the helped; for the helper to push, or persuade, or cajole increases rather than resolves the helped person's ambivalence. For an ambivalent person is like a block checked by a strong spring; the more it is pressed against the spring the stronger the spring becomes, and more and more force will have to be applied to keep it in the desired place. For it to be easily movable the spring must be uncoiled first.

And this is why it is usually true, as a third proposition, that *people need a great deal more help with their negative feelings than with their positive.* They need to look at their negative feelings, to examine them, to discover their weaknesses. Their positive feelings usually get a lot of support. They are acceptable and everyone can weigh in with reassurance, hope, or praise. It's their negative feelings with which they must struggle—their fears, their doubts, their hates, their despair. And this cannot be done, some psychologists and some preachers to the contrary, by pretending that the negative feelings are not there. They are. The man who exhorted us to "accentuate the positive and eliminate the negative" may have discovered a rule of social intercourse but he never had to help people in real trouble—which is why the extroverted, Pollyannaish kind of helper who always wants to keep things pleasant is sometimes more harmful than helpful.

It follows therefore, fourthly, that *the helping relationship must be one in which negative feelings can be expressed without fear of blame, anger, sorrow or loss of face.* This means in turn that it cannot be a relationship of superior and inferior, saint and sinner, wise and foolish, judge and judged, or even their modern equivalent, adjusted and unadjusted. These things may objectively be true, or society may have given one of the pair responsibility to act as if they were true, as in the case of a judge. But as helped and helper struggle together to understand, to come to a point where the helped person makes his decision, they must struggle as equals either of whom could have felt and thought like the other. This is what we mean when we use the rather glib phrases such as "respect for human dignity" and "accepting people as they are"; that both helper and helped are, for all their difference, fallible and imperfect creatures who, if not capable of the particular weaknesses in question, are capable of many others. One of the greatest helpers of delinquent children I ever knew, when I asked once how he was so able to have children share with him their real hopes and fears, said, "Because I have the mind of a criminal myself."

Five other conditions that make possible the commitment to change more or less follow from these four. These are:

5. *The relationship must be centered entirely on the interests of*

the person served.   It cannot be centered in the helper's need to be liked or to control or even to satisfy his own conscience.   It cannot *immediately* be centered on any other good, such as the good of society, the honor of the church or the welfare department, public morality, justice, or fair play, although once real help is given these generally will be added to it.   This is a frequent mistake: to try to kill two birds with one stone and thereby miss them both.   The helped person's need to make his decision is antecedent.   It must come first.

6. *Helping is often helped by limits in which both helper and helped can move.*   To be helped is so frightening that a person can often risk it better if he knows how far it can go, if he is not asked to change altogether, if the power of the helping person is prescribed in some way, by law, by rule, by agreement.   Thus it is helpful for the public assistance recipient to have eligibility requirements; to know that, whatever he may be or what he may confess, that if he is eligible you (hopefully at least) cannot deny him his monthly check. There is help in hospital regulations that, for instance, require a certain length of stay after an operation and do not force a man to make decisions that he can know nothing about.   There is help in agency function, in the helper who can say, "This part of your problem is my business but this part is not."   And there is often help in time, in agreements to try this for so long, or in the approach of a court-hearing or the end of a school year.   You know this yourselves.   The only thing that makes this workshop possible—and helpful to you—is the fact that it will end at four this afternoon. If I said to you, "Come and stay here until you have learned really to be a helping person," you would never come near the place—and quite rightly, too.

7. *It must deal with real things.*   Helping must always deal with real things, however unpleasant.   A doctor who refused to consider cancer of the anus because either he was afraid of cancer or he preferred to ignore the bathroom would be no doctor at all.   So help with social problems must deal with what is really there—with real sorrow, real hate, real sin, and real despair.   It cannot deal with false reassurance, with polite evasions, with "pie in the sky."   And it must deal with them here and now.   It cannot, as in a case I read lately, assure a woman that she ought to be able to get support from an absent husband and do nothing about the fact that her gas and heat were to be turned off that afternoon.

8. *It must be based on trust; on the belief that man can be helped, however wayward he may seem.*   I say this in contradiction to what seems to me the trend in the social sciences today, which progressively appears to see man as sicker and sicker and needing more and more control from his stronger fellows.   But this kind of trust is

necessary if one is to stand by the whole process of helping. Often this is very difficult. Man's first choices in the process of finding himself again are often apparently negative and are in any case quite unpredictable. Thus a grandmother in one case I remember started her recovery and her eventual change from a rigid, denying person into a loving one by beating her granddaughter. If the caseworker had lost faith in the possibility of her changing for the good at that point she might never have come through. The caseworker could not and did not approve of the beating but she could hold to her faith that the grandmother could find in the end a satisfactory relationship and might, in fact, do so not in spite of but because of her mistakes.

9. And finally, and proceeding from this, *it must be based on humility* (in the Christian sense of the word). And this is because in the end you do not know what is right for another (you are lucky indeed if you know it for yourself); you do not have to face what he is facing (and pray God you never may have to); you do not, and you never will, and pray God that you will never try to acquire that pride that dares to assert it does, or even someday may, know the length and the breadth and the depth of a man. Thus I end this list, as I began it, with a paradox. The more you know, the less you know or claim to know.

These conditions for helping are what make me say that to help is a tough proposition, that it needs self-discipline (which is what schools of social work really exist to help you attain); and that prompts me to ask three very impertinent questions which are nevertheless very pertinent:

1. *Do you really want to help?* Do you want to put yourself truly at the service of another, which is not everybody's dish? Or do you in your heart of hearts want to be thanked, or to control, or to ease your own conscience, or to serve some other end? For if you do I do not blame you. There is much else you can do, but helping is not your pigeon.

2. *Are you tough enough to help?* Any idea that helping is a "sissy" business is very far from the truth. It can be, and is, something that calls for every reserve of courage anyone can muster. It takes toughness to face reality, to risk anger, even to court it, to strip the polite veils from sorrow, to allow your clients to make mistakes, to endure their doubts and despair. It takes courage not to disarm them by glossing things over, by being self-righteous, by keeping things on a pleasant and utterly meaningless level.

3. *Are you humble enough to help?* Or, in the last analysis, must people be helped your way, or by you, and you only? Can you say to them and mean it, "There, but for the Grace of God, go I"?

All this, I know, sounds very difficult. It is. But I think that there is help; help for the helper even on a human level. And so, before we go on to look at actual situations I am going to share with you a formulation that I have found helpful, not so much in learning to help as to check on what I am doing whenever I get involved in trying to help. It sounds delightfully simple. It identifies the three things that a helping person needs to convey to a person in trouble. These are:

1. *This is it.* This is the real situation, stripped of all its polite coverings—what you really are up against.

2. *I know that it must hurt.* As far as it is given to me I feel for you and with you in facing this trouble, and any time that you want to bring out your anger, your fear or your doubts it will be acceptable to me—not because I feel them myself but because I could feel them.

3. *I am here if you want me.* I will not force you in any way but at the same time nothing will shake my willingness to help you should you ask it of me.

Simple, yes. Helpful, even. But in the last analysis, nothing that can be given to you, but something that you must make your own.

11

How We Evaluate Our Children*

I WILL BE FRANK to say that the word "evaluate" has negative con-
notations for me. There are two kinds of evaluating that are very
hard to stomach. One is a sitting in judgment on children, a com-
paring of them with some kind of product we have in mind, a
Children's Home Alumnus, and saying in effect, "Child, you are not
worthy of us. You're not worth investing in." And the second is
somewhat alike to it. It is what might be called "competitive evaluation"; it is the sort of evaluation that says that Sally is a finer type of
girl than Sue is and that tries to make our Sues like our Sallies, quite
unmindful of the fact that they are entirely different and equally
valuable people in God's sight if not in ours.

It seems clear that in these instances what we are evaluating is
not a child but ourselves. We may not think that this is what we are
doing but our mind is not on the child at all. It is on *our* reputation;
it is on what *we* would like children to be. It is treating human
beings as a means and not an end, as objects and not as subjects,
and this is the unforgivable sin.

There is a third kind of evaluation, much in vogue today and
much, indeed, preached from the housetops, which also seems to me
to come very near this sin and sometimes, indeed, to commit it.
This is the kind of evaluation made by some psychiatrists and some
social workers that finds out everything it can about a child or his
family, pin-points them, calculates their strengths and their weaknesses, predicts what will become of them and perhaps pins a label to
them, such as "hopeless" or "disturbed," and then acts as if it knew
all about them.

It certainly would be convenient if we could, so as to speak, feed
children into some sort of computer and then know exactly what we
were dealing with. But the danger of this sort of thing seems to be
not only that it is presumptuous, and therefore partakes of the nature
of the first of all the deadly sins, but, in less theological language, it
underrates children and institutions, too. Either it denies actually
that we can be really helpful agencies that can produce real change in
people, and makes of us simply a sort of cold-frame in which children
are reared with little recognition that our mission is not so much to
rear as to bring change and growth to the broken, or it calls on us to

* Given to the Presbyterian Association of Children's Homes, Barium
Springs, N.C., April 1960.

do the whole job of changing without recognizing the part in this that the child and his family have to play.

We may, some of us, find some uneasiness in being called on to recognize both our responsibility and our aloneness here. It is much easier simply to rear. And of course, rear we must. But increasingly in our society this is becoming a minor role and the strength of the church is being called on to be something more than a substitute parent. It is being called on to heal and to save. And yet at the same time helping is much more than becoming that somewhat cold-sounding entity, a "treatment center."

The institution needs perhaps first of all to be a place where children who have been let down by life learn again to trust adults, other children, and themselves. It needs to be a place where children and their families can get themselves back in the stream of meaningful living where people matter to each other and life has content once again. And to this end I believe that the institution, which went through a period of being despised and depreciated, is particularly adapted, through its tangible, firm structure, its flexibility, so that it can permit children to relearn relationship at their own speed and with a wide choice of people to relate to, and because when the institution is church related or church centered it stands for something in this life and the next.

But this needs to be added: that whatever the problem is, a child or an adult cannot get help for it until he finds something with which he can become positively or negatively engaged, which he can use to bring about change in himself. This was as true in 1940 as it will be in 1970.

This brings me back to evaluation, and in particular to the static kind of evaluation that sometimes passes for understanding. It makes clear that the real question that we have to ask, is, not so much, "What is this child like? Is he good or bad, strong or weak?" but, "Can this child, or can his family, make use of what we have to give?"—along with which goes always a second question: "Can we make it available to him?"

What we have to give is what our institutions are. And there are clearly some children, and some families, too, about which we can quite properly make the sort of diagnosis that I have spoken about. We can quite properly say, I think, that there is little chance of some children being able to make use of what we have to give simply because the things that we have are more or less adapted to children who can go to school and who must live together in groups. Thus it would be hard for a child of very low I.Q. or one whose behavior was dangerous to others around him to make use of what we have, although this does not remove from us the obligation to consider from time to time whether we could not adapt our program somewhat to make it possible to include some children we now reject.

But these are more or less gross judgments. The more subtle, and the more difficult, situation arises when we have a child of more or less normal intelligence, perhaps even of some promise, perhaps of some ability to conform to our way of life, who does, perhaps, one of two things. In adolescence he may seem to become surly, indifferent to our attempts to help him, and end not so much in re-belling against us as in disregarding the rules that we have made for his safety. Maybe he begins slipping out at night, and we finally have to dismiss him. Or, although he stays with us, he becomes very dependent, indecisive, unambitious and ends by going into service so as to continue being looked after, or, if a girl, rushes too quickly into marriage.

There are more of both kinds of tragedy than we like to think about. Sometimes we blame ourselves for this. We begin to fear that we misjudged him in the first place, or that we don't have the right kind of program for adolescents. We fear that we have kept him too long, or that there is more to this "institutionalization" business than we have been willing to allow. Or, if our tendency is to lay blame outside ourselves, and some of us are adepts at this, we begin to wonder if there is not more to heredity than we have been told, or maintain that we did not have him long enough, or that we could have done something with him if his parents had not interfered (despite the fact that he is only too often the child with little family tie).

There are of course, many reasons, both inside and outside our programs, why things may go right or wrong. All these reasons may be more or less true. They do not however explain fully why some children succeed and others do not. What really makes the dif-ference between the child who fulfills expectations and the one who does not is the quality of his engagement with us—whether in fact he lives with us or merely exists in our place. And here we meet a paradox. This quality of being engaged, of being willing to take help, is both something that we can do something about and some-thing that we can not. That is, we can make it possible, by the way that we treat the child, by our program or our policies, but in the end the decision to get help or not to get it is one that only the child can make.

Perhaps this can be illustrated by recounting a discussion I had in an institution recently with five young girls, aged eight to sixteen. We were discussing, with, I hasten to say, the administration's per-mission and indeed blessing, what living there was like. In the course of our discussion the children brought up why they were there. It began with Alice, who had been complaining that her housemother did not trust her, denying the importance of what she had just said. She was not here on the same terms as the other children; she could leave at any time. Immediately Alice's behavior that had puzzled her housemother began, as it were, to expose its roots. Alice was terribly untidy. She went about with a tear in her dress. She took little care of herself. Her lips were chapped and she would not put any salve on them. Talking with her it became clear that Alice was saying that she would not let the Home take care of her in any way. The salve was the Home's. She would not use it. So were needles and houseparents who would help one mend a dress. Alice was denying in fact that she belonged in the Home at all—that either its rules or its kindness had any meaning for her.

This got the other children talking. Linda, whose housemother found her moody and often prickly in her relationships, swore that her mother could make a home for her but that her step-father did not want her. She made it clear that this was only to be expected. Step-fathers were people who did not care. But Linda was living under an illusion; she could not admit to herself that it was her mother who did not care, and as a result she was suspicious of any-one who wanted to like her and anyone that she felt that she liked. Linda, however, was on the way to finding a more meaningful life because there was one thing and one person she was willing to trust. These were the pastor and the Church. As we came away from the meeting she said to me that she felt safe with the pastor because one could always trust the Church. The Home really did have a chance to help her through the relationship she would permit herself with one part of its life.

Jackie chimed in next. Her pattern of life had been one of struggling against rules, of getting spanked or put on restriction. She was able to meet her problem only by blaming the Home. Her parents, she said, could care for her and wanted to, but the Home had demanded of them an impossible standard of stability and be-havior. I have some hopes for Jackie. Although her engagement with the Home was of a negative nature there was something real about it—her recognition of the difference between the Home's standards and those of her parents. She will need help in accepting the Home's standards, but we do so often find that it is the rebellious child, the one with whom we have had the most run-ins, who in the end can witness more sincerely than any other to what they got from the Home.

We heard then from the smallest of the group. Here was a child so timid and shy that the housemother had told me that it was no use trying to talk with Christine. She would never open her mouth. She did, as she dissolved in tears, as she wailed that she did not

know why she was there at all. All this had happened to her and
she was utterly overwhelmed by it.

It remained for Joanne, the oldest, and the most secure child of
the lot, to say frankly that there were many things that she did not
like at the Home, but she had nowhere else to go, and she was
determined to make the most of what she had.

Now to some extent the difference between these children lay in
what the Home had done to them, the way in which it had been able
to help them face reality and the understanding that it had shown
them. But also there was something in the way each child had
tackled the problem. Of the five Alice, who denied everything, and
Christine, who accepted too much, had the least capacity for relationship. Unless something can be done to help them they are the
likely candidates for trouble later on.

What does this kind of insight tell us about what we should look
for, both in children coming to us and those which we already have?
I think it lays stress not so much on what a child is but on what he
is doing about the way he has been hurt. All five of these girls had
been hurt. They had been let down by the adults around them.
They were handling it in different ways, some realistically, some
through illusion, some through struggling against the truth. One
could know a tremendous lot about their use of the Home without
knowing their IQ's or their heredity, although this knowledge might
also have been helpful to us.

So these are some of the questions I would like to ask about
children before they come to the Home and at intervals afterwards.
Before they come I would like to ask, not are they well behaved, or
intelligent, or obedient but do they show any evidence of being really
related to people? Can they share with the caseworker or the
superintendent their real fears and doubts about coming to the Home?
Are they over-compliant, crushed like poor little Christine was, with
the weight of what was happening to her? I do not doubt that
Christine made a very good impression as she was studied for ad-
mission. I am sure they found her obedient, accepting, neatly dressed
and probably with the sweet, sad smile she still showed. She was so
crushed that she could not be herself.

Or are they unreal, as Alice was, about the terms and conditions
on which they will live at the home—for Alice's dream of being able
to go home anytime she wanted to was exactly that, a dream? Have
their parents been—or can they be—honest with them about why,
and how long, they will have to stay? Have they, as many children
have, been promised something they cannot have—what I call the
Great Horse Myth—the pony for every child; and if so, do they believe it? Or do they believe that other myth—the Myth of the Six-
Inch Strap? And of a child who has been with you for a while I

would ask: Has he been able to form any kind of a close relationship with anyone on the campus—with his housemother, or work supervisor, or the pastor or the janitor? Is there anyone he can trust? Does he show some real interest in something, however humble this may be? It is where a child is not involved, either positively or negatively, that I would begin to worry.

There is, of course, much that we can do to help a child become involved. We can have an interesting program and worthwhile people in his life. We can be honest with him. We can show him that we understand. But we can also do much not only to test out how much he can relate but to help him understand what is happening to him by the way in which we work with him before he comes to us. This, I would say, much more than "finding out about him," is what a good social worker can do. It is helping him find himself. I do not pretend it is all the answer. But I would respond to the question that is implicit in the title that you gave me to discuss: How do we evaluate our children? by saying that what we need to evaluate is not so much our children, or even ourselves, but how the two are working together and indeed whether they can do so.

No matter how good our programs are, they are sterile unless we can help people use them. We obviously do not know all about it—what makes some children and families able to change and grow and what hinders others from doing so. Psychology and psychiatry are helpful but they do not know either. They cannot give us a whole answer. Good procedures, careful planning, what social workers call good structure, are also helpful, but not the whole solution. The problem lies somewhere in the spirit of man, in his will and in the way we respond to it. And I think that we in the church, using all the knowledge that the world can give us, have as good a chance as any of learning what it is that helps and hinders, for it is essentially in this kind of revitalizing of broken spirits that we should be concerned. It is what Grace and redemption are about.

In the meantime let us watch this factor of involvement, shall we, and do what we can to give it an honest chance to grow.

12

Casework Is a Practical Activity*

IN ALL TOO MANY institutions casework is not fulfilling the real needs of children. Nor are the caseworkers doing casework, but a sort of last-minute rescuing of situations which, with good casework, ought never to have developed. It is true that up to the time when the child enters the institution there is casework being done in helping the child and his parents come to terms with the institution's service and begin to use it. But all too often after the child is in care what we have is something quite different.

This situation can perhaps be best understood in terms of the difference between casework and counseling, as set forth in an article some years ago by Herbert Aptekar. Casework in this definition, is concerned with a tangible, practical service, and is the method by which the client is related to the service and makes his decision whether, and how, he can use it. Counseling, on the other hand, is a service whose primary emphasis is the client's "problem," or confusion, or upsettedness, which can be treated more or less independently of tangible or practical services. Psychotherapy, a third method of help, deals with changes in personality itself. In actual fact, because of priorities and because there are many puzzling and puzzled children in institutions, we all to often have caseworkers doing "casework," a practical, understandable function, with the child before he comes to the institution and when he is ready to leave it. But while the child is in the institution, what do we have? Not "casework"—although there may be some casework around practical things such as parental visiting—but most generally "counseling" directed towards children who are showing "problem." To the houseparent and to the child, therefore, the main purpose of the caseworker becomes a counseling function when difficulty arises.

This type of service starts with many strikes against it. It is hard to explain. It comes at a time of apparent failure, so that housemothers feel a little ashamed that their children need "social service" and the child recognizes that his behavior has singled him out for attention. It is discontinuous, because it involves a new relationship at the point of crisis, and it can never either be allowed to be entirely voluntary (if the child is troubled he needs casework help) or imposed (one cannot use counseling help unless one is willing to make

* Reprinted, with some alterations, from *Welfare News*, Raleigh, N.C., December 1955.

use of it). It is something which is not the prerogative of social work—the minister, the superintendent, the housemother, the football coach also "counsel" and sometimes with more pertinence to the child's present situation. It has, moreover, a disintegrating effect as it removes the social service department from the ordinary life of the institution and makes of it a kind of expert intrusion into cottage and day-to-day life.

"Casework," as distinguished from "counseling," is, or should be a practical everyday activity. Only as such can it ever be in an institution, rather than attached to it, and be accepted as such. What then, are the practical things around which the social service staff should be operating? Genevieve Johnson, in an article published as long ago as 1950, lists casework activities, which, if possibly not always too well defined, often have this quality of practicality. These examples come from the relationships that she entitled "Activity with Children":

Discussing with Sharon the things she would like to say to her father in an anticipated telephone call.

Around an intergroup transfer for eight-year-old Mary, helping her pull together a list of questions she wanted to discuss with her prospective housemother; later, introducing the housemother to Mary in the former's room, helping them get started together; still later, knowing from Mary how the introductory interview went.

Hearing from Philip of his concern over his mother's not visiting, her present whereabouts, her progress in the hospital; letting him know that we would look to planning a visit to her.

Helping Bill encompass an unexpected transfer from one school to another.

Although Miss Johnson also "counsels," she can be seen to be related to certain everyday aspects of institutional life, not only with regard to the parent-child relationship, an area long claimed by casework, but to such things as cottage and school transfers. To these might be added such things as work assignments, relations with clothing sponsors (if such a system is used), perhaps even management of the clothing budget, extracurricular participation or opportunities, visits outside the institution, etc., in fact the whole matrix of decision about the child which affects his life in the institution as a whole. The caseworker does not need to be the deciding person in each case—for instance, work assignments may need to be decided by a committee of houseparent, work supervisor, and caseworker— but she does need to be the person with whom the child discusses these decisions, comes to accept them or battle against them, and is helped adjust to them.

Why? There would seem to be a number of reasons, of which three are very important.

1. These are the "battle-grounds" of the placed child. A few very vocal children are able to verbalize distress around more or less abstract "problems." Most express their feeling around much more practical issues.

2. Only through experiencing help around little and fairly "safe" issues can the child learn to trust the caseworker on larger, more threatening issues. Who would be more able to turn to the caseworker for help—Mary, who has experienced the caseworker's help in effecting a cottage transfer, or a Margaret, not named by Miss Johnson but all too real in practice, who is confronted by a relative stranger at a time when her feelings are already torn up and hostile?

3. Casework is a practical activity and should be seen as such. Which is the housemother likely to want to work with—the person whose job is defined and understandable, with whom she is accustomed to have her children do practical things, just as they do practical things with the coach or the work supervisor, or a person who comes to talk with the child about those very nebulous things called "feelings"?

Such a function for the caseworker does not preclude counseling. Indeed it makes it more possible and far less threatening. It calls, of course, for some understanding of the help that casework can be in everyday life on the part of the administration and some coming down to earth on the part of the caseworker whose concept of her own function is rarefied or superior. Such a relationship saves the hours that now are spent in somewhat unproductive attempts to establish a counseling relationship with the troubled child. Moreover, good counselors are rare—rarer, even, than the competent caseworker.

While the outcome of the case is still unknown, the possible involvement of a social service department in a specific case illustrates this difference. Margaret, 11, is creating problems in her cottage. She has two siblings—Thelma, 17, who appears to be a stable youngster, and Wayne, 7, who worries the social service staff because he is so withdrawn. The trouble seems to lie in the promises made by the children's mother, who is always on the point of taking the children home but never does so. Work with the mother, at a distance, seems not to be too successful.

The conventional "counseling" approach would be to try to work with Margaret directly, since she is the one in trouble, and perhaps try some environmental change (or even counseling) with Wayne. At once, in Margaret's case, one runs into difficulties. Margaret will not talk. She does not want to come to social service. The housemother either presses her, since she is pretty desperate, but is not sure about what Margaret will get from the experience, or resists Margaret's coming. The caseworker-counselor can only tell Margaret that she wants to help her—Margaret must be unhappy or she would not behave so badly. Maybe Margaret is so unhappy that she can finally ask for help. The chances are, to be brutally frank, that with the probable skill of the caseworker, the probable vagueness about this service, or resistance of the housemother, plus Margaret's natural defensiveness, very little will happen.

But what if the caseworker's acknowledged role is not so much that of a counselor or a trouble-shooter but is more that of a person concerned with practical situations? What is he likely to do? Why, consult with Thelma, the older sister, about family plans and their effect on the younger children. This will seem natural both to Thelma and her housemother. Later, if Margaret needs help, it can be given from a background of practical action already taken rather than as springing from Margaret's misbehavior.

Casework is not counseling. It is not a mysterious dealing with feelings *per se*. It is a skilled but nevertheless understandable method of making available perfectly ordinary services and of helping a person come to terms with life through what he experiences in making use of them. Casework is first and foremost a practical activity.

Casework also, if it is integrated into the day to day service of the institution, has a preventive role by meeting problems before they arise.

Recently one institution has taken steps in this direction. Recognizing that many children go through a very difficult stage between their thirteenth and fifteenth birthdays, when they begin to face the fact that they are likely to spend four or five years more under care, the institution does not wait until they get into trouble. It uses the occasion of the thirteenth birthday to call the child in and review with him what has gone on in the past and what is likely in the future. Again, although there is not as yet enough evidence on which to base a theory, preliminary results would seem to show that these children face the future with a great deal more clarity, and that if they get into trouble later they will meet their caseworker not as one associated with the trouble but as one with whom they have been working all the time.

13.

Some Problems in the Spiritual Training of Children in Group Care*

THE SPIRITUAL TRAINING of children means more than helping them just to be good, or kind, or loving, important as these things are. For the purpose of this paper, at least, it means helping children come into a relationship with their living Lord. It means helping them believe in (that is, put their trust in) God. It means helping them arrive at the state where they want to be kind and good not because they will be punished or unpopular if they are not, not because goodness and kindness "pays off," but out of love and gratitude to the God who nurtures and has redeemed them. The beginning of wisdom may be the fear of the Lord, but fear in this context is best translated by "awe" or "reverence." The mature Christian responds to God in love, awe and gratitude but not by being "afraid," in the ordinary sense of the word.

Quite clearly then what we are talking about is more than ethics and more than going to church or Sunday School. We are not talking here about how to instruct children in the Bible or in theology, both of which, of course, need to de done. We are concerned rather with their attitude toward what they learn and their ability to make it part of their lives.

The child-care institution which is rooted in the church, and often the one that isn't, is naturally concerned that children be helped all they can in this. Often they are very well staffed with practicing Christians skilled in teaching the Word. They have facilities and a routine which should contribute to understanding. Frequently much that they say and do is expressed in religious terms. The names of God, of Jesus are not confined to church on Sundays. They do not have to struggle with what many of us who teach outside are faced with—the non-attender or the child who never hears God mentioned

* Summary of a Session with houseparents at the North Carolina Association of Child Caring Institutions, September 1960. Reprinted in *News-n-Views*, September-October 1960, and in slightly revised form, in the *Chapel Hill Workshop Reports*, Part I, 1961.

except in a Sunday School class.   At first glance it might seem that
the institution's is an easy task.

But it is not.   I would like to suggest, in fact, that there are four
important reasons why this is not so.

1. Children learn about God through their human experience.
Ineffable as is God's relationship to us, we have no other way of
expressing it than to compare it to the nearest human relationship
that seems to have some of the same quality.   We call Him our
Father.   But it would be very hard to get even a glimpse of what
God's Fatherhood meant if "Father" means to you someone who
gets drunk and beats you.   Nor is this simply a matter of words.
It is hard to know what forgiveness means if you have never really
been forgiven.   Thus the children's own past experiences of relationship are something that have to be understood.

2. Since the basis of faith is "trust"—in a person, not a proposition—we have to reckon with the fact that "trust" is what these children have lost.   The children who come to an institution have been
let down by life as they know it.   They have no reason to trust.   They
have lost their trust in adults, since their own parents have failed
them.   They have lost trust in themselves.   The unanswered, implicit
question that is in the mind of every child who is cared for away from
home is, "What is wrong with me that this has happened to me?
Why am I different?   Is it my fault?"   And they have lost trust in
Providence.   Why should they trust in an all-loving God when, to
their minds at least, life has been cruel to them?   The problem of
human suffering is one of the hardest for a mature Christian to face.
The Book of Job spends forty-two chapters exploring it and comes up
with the answer that the mystery is "too wonderful" to understand.
How should a child find a ready answer?

Some do, of course.   A little girl recently told me that in her
bewilderment in all the new relationships that had been thrust upon
her there was one thing she could trust—the Church.   But she was,
I think, exceptional in that she had this concept before she had to
leave home.   Other children are not so fortunate.   We have to help
them to this faith.

3. Children often fight to protect themselves from the realization
that their parents do not love them by denying that this is so, and
blaming the institution for judging their parents and keeping them
away from them.   Although some children may be grateful for the
care that they are receiving we are all too familiar with the opposite.
In the children's minds the institution is all too often intent on
showing up their parents; the very fact that the care it gives is
superior feels like a judgment and it makes it harder for the child
to admit the fact that he was unloved at home.   And since the institution obviously cares about religion, the child may identify religion

with his struggle against the institution. In fact he may find in religion the institution's most sensitive spot. He can show his independence, yes, and get his own back more, by denying what those around him care the most about.

4. Religion, when it is preached on what might be called its negative side, its prohibitions and condemnations, both reinforces the guilt that he has for what has happened to his family and reinforces his unwilling judgment on them—the very things he is trying to deny.

Recently I had occasion to ask four questions of a number of children in institutions. I asked them first whether they believed that God loved them even when they were bad, and whether they thought God wanted them to be happy. To my joy they were unanimous in claiming God's mercy for themselves. But when it came to questions that touched on their parents' problems there was much more ambivalence and their uneasiness was apparent. Over half the younger ones thought that God punished people by making them sick or even by killing them. It is true that some Old Testament stories would suggest this but I fear for those of our children whose firmest impression of Grace is this. Again, about half of the younger children thought that the commission of a specific sin—in this case drinking—condemned their parents to Hell, although the older ones had some sense of God's forgiveness given to all. I quote these instances not to criticize the way in which religion had been taught to them but to emphasize how easily children whose parents are obvious sinners can catch hold of a one-sided interpretation and make their own problem worse.

How can we help these children? One cannot, of course, make a person religious. There are no rules, no methods. But if children are to get a glimpse of what religion may mean to them, if ever they are to regain the kind of trust in others and in themselves that will make it possible for them to put their trust in God, this may come about because of the way in which we ourselves conceive of and trust in God, and the way in which we translate this into our treatment of those about us. (This is, of course, asking ourselves how we fulfill the Great Commandment in both of its parts.) And, if I may, I would like to suggest some questions we might ask ourselves.

1. *Is the Gospel really "Good-News" to us?* Is our own religion something that matters to us and fills us with joy? Do our faces lighten on Easter Sunday and do we convey to our children that this is something important to us? This seems to me the only answer to religion's unfortunate tendency to become just another of the Home's activities, like school or the work program.

Some time ago I was discussing church attendance with some children in an institution. They were complaining that church attendance was "required" and thought that this would not happen in an own family. I pointed out that I "expected" my son and daughter to attend church and Sunday School every Sunday. The children jumped on the difference in terms. To them there was something quite different in being "expected" and "required" to attend church, even though the results were the same. The first implied that church was important, the second that it was routine. The difference may seem very subtle but to the children it was not.

2. *Do we, in discussing religion, present a picture of a living, forgiving Lord?* Of all of God's children these, who carry such a burden of guilt, need to know Him as Savior. They need what one church calls, "The comforts of our holy religion." In a Home which is full of new and rather exacting rules (to them) they need principally not a greater sense of how narrow and strait the gate but how wide is God's mercy, His "steadfast love" towards his creatures. And this leads me to a third question:

3. *Do we use religion to enforce adult discipline?* While we would all, I think, want to use God's Word as the ultimate touchstone, and the life of Jesus as the ultimate example, it is very easy for some of us to use religion to reinforce our quite secular demands on the child's behavior. This is not fair, especially when our demand is not really a matter of moral significance, but a matter of keeping order, or one of the normal socialization of the child. For a child to feel that God is always on the side of the adults in the child's struggle with adult expectations—even, let us say, in the matter of keeping his room tidy or in table manners—is to make of Him quite the wrong kind of Father. Joe Louis was once asked, early in World War II, whether God was on our side. He replied, "I don't know. But I hope that we are on His."

4. *When we talk of sin, do we include ourselves as sinners?* I do not mean that we should present ourselves to the child as any worse than we are, but it is, I think, important that we not present ourselves as wholly good. The child needs to know that we are human, too, and equally in need of God's Grace. Indeed, we cannot really help him unless we are conscious that under different circumstances we could have done what he has done. Father Brown, in G. K. Chesterton's delightful detective stories, is able to unravel crime by putting himself in the criminal's place—feeling that he could be tempted to do the same if he felt this or that pressure on him. Nothing helps us to accept our fellows for what they are and really to love them as much as a sense of our common sinfulness—there, but for the Grace of God, go I—and nothing is harder to live with than a person who presents himself as wholly righteous—witness the Pharisees. The housemother who can occasionally apologize to the child for a too hasty decision or who can tell him sincerely that she can understand how hard it was for him to try to fight temptation is on the way to

helping him join the fellowship of those who walk humbly with their God.

5. *Do we make of our cottage devotions a joyous, participating thing,* in which all children—the refractory, the inarticulate, the childish, the stupid as well as the well-adjusted and the articulate can participate? Talking with children I have found that they often equate leadership in such devotions with adult approval, as if religion were a prerequisite of the righteous and successful. It is the others who need it most.

6. *Can we forgive?* Because we are so much with the child, because we are used to looking at his development and growth with interest and concern, and may even keep records on his behavior, we often forget that the central message of the Gospel is forgiveness. Children need punishment, yes, but not to remain in an unforgiven state. I was recently talking to a child who had been pretty ungovernable for a while and had been on the "chain-gang" (the Saturday morning work detail for those breaking certain rules) for three or four weeks at a time. Then, by rather considerable effort, he had kept himself off for seven weeks. The eighth week he slipped. When he reported for "sentencing" the administrator treated him as a habitual delinquent whereas he saw himself as having improved a great deal. He felt that his past punishments had in no way led to "wiping the slate clean" and I wonder how he could know what forgiveness is.

This factor has much to do with my dislike, which is growing, against the habit of punishing children by campusing them or restricting them over long periods of time. There are children in our institutions who remain on restriction a great part of the time, or who are "off restriction" and on again in an alternation as regular as day and night. To these our efforts at discipline cease to be a chastening love and become a constant denial of what little freedom any institution can give.

What teaching children spiritual values calls for, in short, is more than a knowledge of the scriptures, more than personal piety and more than good teaching technique. It calls for us to practice in the limited way that we can the kind of love God has for us—that love that is always concerned for us even when it chastens, and that hates sin but obstinately goes on loving the sinner.

14.

How Successful Are We in Handling Children's Sexual Growth?

THIS IS A difficult subject. Even to talk on the problem is to get oneself tarred, if only so slightly, with the brush of those who favor more permissiveness, more freedom in sexual behavior, and even to be thought a disciple of that terrible fellow, Freud. And those who object have good reason for questioning this doctrine. It has certainly not gone along with an age noted for its sexual morality. One might even wonder when someone is going to talk on sex at a meeting such as this and stress the need for more controls.

I have every sympathy for any one of you who is thinking in this way. And yet I believe that this is not the real problem. The problem about sex is not a quantitative one. Shall we have more or less of it? Shall we express it or repress it? It is a qualitative one. What kind of a relationship do we want our children to have, both now and in the future, with what is called the "opposite" sex? And only by answering, "None" can we avoid the problem.

This is, perhaps, using "sex" in a broader sense than the world as a whole uses it; which was, as a matter of fact, one of the social errors that Freud made and which led to so much misunderstanding of what he was trying to say. For in this I think he was right, not in his emphasis on sex but in his understanding that there was not a separate impulse, connected only with procreation, which was at one and the same time both holy and greatly to be deplored. There was, and is, a relationship between the sexes which is indissolubly interwoven into the process of growing up. It starts with mother and father love, and is different for boys than it is for girls. It continues, sometimes in nearness and sometimes in opposition, throughout the formative years and has a lot to do with finding one's role in life, and it cumulates in adult love and responsible marriage. It is also holy, but in quite another sense—not holy because it is something to be held out of this world, but holy because it is God's ordinance—male and female created He them. And I find it significant that the story of Genesis does not emphasize sexual union as a special act, not, at least, until after the Fall. Eve was created as a companion, not a mistress.

In other words total maturity and sexual maturity go together. The immature person is sexually immature; the sexually immature are wholly immature at heart. The trouble with our age, and particularly the sexual trouble with our age is not so much lust as another of the seven deadly sins, gluttony, or the failure to be responsible or to discriminate. It is lack of taste. This seems to me obvious not only in the irresponsibility of divorce for trivial reasons, not only in the irresponsibility of bringing illegitimate children into the world for the sake of a moment's pleasure, but in the kind of sex which is the American ideal, the whipped-cream, mooing calf-love sort of love of television and the magazine story, which, moreover, justifies any sort of irresponsible behavior because one happens to fall in "love." This to me is more serious than the few occasions of preoccupation with the physical that goes under the name of lust, although I realize the two are sometimes connected, and that the social results of lust can be terrible indeed.

To find oneself in the world of men and women, to know what love is like, to be able to give and take affection responsibly, to use God's gift of communication through touch, and eye, and word and His delight in beauty and not to misuse it—these seem to me the things that we should strive for. These are things which are the preparation for a mature, responsible life and a mature responsible love, one that "doth not behave itself unseemly; seeketh not her own; is not easily provoked."

What is this to do with children's institutions or with our primary question, our success or failure in handling children's sexual growth? Simply this: that I think too often we have considered sex as something that could be handled separately, away from our main problem of helping children grow to maturity. We have not considered how our general treatment of children affects their sexual growth, or, conversely, how what we do in the area of sex relationship (which we all too often pigeon-hole as "boy-girl relations") affects, or may even undo, what we strive for as a whole.

I don't want to minimize the difficulties of bringing children up in groups, nor the anxieties incumbent on being responsible for other people's children. I don't want to discount the fact that many of these children come from families which, to say the least, have not been distinguished by their sexual morality. And I am only too well aware that most of us, myself included, are subjected to pressures, both external and internal, from a heritage which has all too often considered there to be only one deadly sin, with the possible exception of certain manifestations of the sin of sloth. One might wonder, parenthetically, what would have happened if we had paid equal attention to anger, envy, pride and avarice, and if our present civilization did not consider gluttony, both in sex and in economic consumption, something of a virtue.

But I wish that this were one of the areas in which I felt that one could honestly talk as one of you says about what is right about institutions. I think you all know that I do think that a lot of things are right about institutions and any comments I may make are made in a context of love.

But I will have to say, frankly, that this is an area in which we all have something to learn. And as I visit institutions—not all, but some—these four manifestations cause me some uneasiness:

First, the fear that so many of our children express about their relationships with the other sex, and their awareness that they find it hard to discriminate between the good and the bad in them. Part of this may be just a good argument on the children's part to plead for more liberal dating policies, but it is too general to be entirely this. The fear is a real one, and it is borne out too often by early and somewhat unwise marriage after leaving us.

Secondly, although we have, I think, done better in this in the last few years, many children in institutions act below their sexual age. I don't mean at all that they are unsophisticated. That is nice. But children of eleven or twelve often seek affection, sometimes on a physical level and often despite the housemother's frowns as if they were six or seven, and those of six and seven as if they were three.

But, of course, you say, these are deprived children who did not receive enough affection before they came to the Home. True. Nevertheless there is a definite relation between the kind of care that the Home is giving and this retardation. I still remember with embarrassment, because I had to refuse their request and because it was so earnest, of a group of fourteen-year old girls in an institution noted for its high moral tone, to cuddle up on my knee, and how, in the same institution, ten and eleven year old boys seemed confused about their sex and acted like little girls. How are these boys and girls ever to make a mature relationship, if their basic relationships with a father are so far below their age? What kind of marriage partners are they likely to look for and how can they be partners and not children all their lives?

Thirdly, I think we have too much homosexuality in institutions to be entirely happy with ourselves. Some of this may be real sickness but all too often it comes because we have been so discouraging of normal sexual contacts.

And, lastly, I am concerned because we have, in a negative way, placed so much emphasis on sex. We have made "smooching" an all too desirable form of revolt. We have apparently convinced all too many of our children that our lack of trust in them—a thing which all adolescents complain of, but which institutional adolescents feel more deeply than anyone else—is at bottom a sexual fear. Too many children, in my experience, interpret rules and regulations which are simply matters of order as suspicion of what they might do if a boy and a girl should be together and they would not do so if someone, maybe the housemother, maybe the administration, did not feel it to be so. I still remember the boy who told me that he felt "watched" wherever he went. He found himself one day with a girl and was sure that nobody was watching. "I didn't like her much," he said, "but I had to do something to celebrate and so I grabbed her and kissed her." What are the chances that if there had been an unseen watcher the boy would have been had on the carpet for smooching and not for asserting his independence by breaking a rule?

Many institutions have done a great deal in the last few years to tackle the problem. Some have been, and are, fearful. Let us be clear what the problem is. It is not a matter of encouraging or for-bidding liberties between the sexes. As one of you said to another last year, "Why, you seem to encourage what we are trying to stop." It is rather a matter of recognizing what is normal and healthy and *useful* to a child, whether this be holding hands or having a father's knee to sit on or to know how to manage a date, and what is silly, or dangerous or unhealthy. It is a matter of helping a child find what is good and what is bad in this bewildering two-sex world, or of forcing him to discover it on his own later when a mistake will really hurt. Childhood is, and should be a time of safe experimentation, within limits, and under control.

It can't be so if we insist that the problem isn't there, that the relationship between the sexes is a problem that should be ignored by the healthy child. I know this from bitter experience. I come from a culture in which sex is not recognized to exist in anyone under eighteen. In all too many cases the result is twisted relationships and that pathetic substitute, homosexualty. And this is in a culture that de-emphasizes sex, while our own glorifies it. And it can't be done by trying to repress any move towards the other sex, in the fear that being together will lead to holding hands, and holding hands to kissing, and kissing to seduction. As one child said to me recently, "The crime in this institution is not what one does with a girl. It is being with her. If they caught us together and didn't see us smooch-ing, they'd assume either that we had just finished or hadn't had time yet to begin."

What then ought we to do about it? Nothing, if we don't want to. Perhaps rather little as long as our Boards and our constituencies share our fears. But I do think we could break down somewhat the invisible wall some institutions maintain between the boys' and the girls' side of campus, or the invisible wall that some cottages have drawn around themselves. We can do much with common playgrounds, teen-age centers, committees. Some of you know my predilection for the family cottage. I have just returned from a Home which has never had any other way of living, and there's no doubt in my mind, both from this and other experiences, that there is a great relaxation of the problem where this is the rule.

I was in one of these cottages once when something happened which illustrates more clearly than anything I can say one part, at least of the problem. A twelve or thirteen year-old boy pinched an eleven-year old girl's seat. Now maybe we shouldn't have subjected him to this temptation, and I agree it was temptation. The girl was bending over and she had on shorts. Or maybe the housemother should have taken the boy aside and pointed out how bad it was to give in to such an impulse. But Bob learned in a more constructive way. Jenny turned and slapped his face. I asked Jenny afterwards if she had much trouble, and she said, "Oh, he's new. I'll soon have him in hand." How much better was it for Jenny to learn in an uncomplicated way how to deal with unwelcome liberties at the age of eleven than it was to be protected from them?

But of course any such arrangement needs strong leadership in the cottage. Where such experiments have gone wrong this has been the trouble. The Jennys must not be left with problems which they cannot cope with or which have gotten out of hand. But strong leadership in a cottage does not mean a rigid control. It is a fact that rather more sex delinquencies occur in homes with over-strict backgrounds than do in those which are too lax, and rather few in between.

The most successful houseparent that I know in this realm, and at that in a one-sex cottage, is that because she can identify with the culture of teen-agers, one might almost say their needs, and yet be firm on limits. She can kid her girls about holding hands with their boy-friends and yet be direct with them when there is any danger of them stepping over the line. But she could not do it unless her administration was behind her.

This is too large a problem for us to tackle today—how we can help houseparents be wise leaders, who know that leadership cannot be all likeness and not all difference, but must be part of each. Perhaps we ought to start with ourselves. Do we really believe that there is something good and natural that a child ought to experience, something perhaps a little more than just being acquainted with the other sex and its ways from a respectful distance, that will provide them with some strength both against temptation and against the more subtle debasing of sex? Or do we think of sex as something that, whatever its eventual purpose, should be scotched in children wherever it raises its ugly head? Or do we perhaps, although recognizing its positive and its negative aspects, remain so afraid of the latter that we are willing to forgo the former? Do we act with prudent caution or with blind fear? And do we know much about it? I have been impressed lately with our lack of understanding of the part that sex relationships play in the social life of the teenager, and how we have sometimes given specifically sexual significance, on the level of love or passion, to social conveniences such as "going steady" or the last-minute "date" to a school party, which are sometimes the protection that this bewildering culture throws up to prevent itself from being hurried into too serious an affair.

I have tried to give you some of my feeling about this problem and some of my observations. I do not pretend to be an expert, and certainly I do not have the job of running an institution myself. I hope you will challenge me on it. Because it is an important matter. It is not just a question of indulging children's demands. It is a much more important thing, not only for the child's future, for his growth to maturity, but for his whole attitude, now and in the future, towards himself and towards the gifts with which he has been endowed of God.

A Devotional*

WE ARE KNOWN as children of God; and it seems to me very pertinent that those of us who are parents and teachers of children should ponder what that means. For I am fully convinced that if we want to understand human relationships we must look to that other Relationship on which all our lives depend.

Our being His children means, of course, that He provides for us. It means that He chastens us when we need it. It means that He will forgive us. He does not continue in anger against us. If we need Him, He is there.

It means that He offers Himself to us, not as an indulgent father who will smooth our path for us and protect us from all pain, but as Someone we can trust and rely on, Who loves us enough to trust us to experience joy and pain. He will never exploit us or use us for personal ends of His own. He cares so much for us that He has left us free to choose whether and how we shall use Him. He seeks us constantly but never engulfs us with His love, never demands that we accept it. It is the devil who devours a man, absorbs him, makes him like himself, but God graciously invites us to partake of Him if we wish.

It is, in fact, one of the marvels of God's amazing love for us that He respects us. He listens to us. He allows us to be different from each other and from Him, and despite what we are, He thinks that we are worth something. The great distinction in the Bible is not between being a child and being a man, but between being a son and being a servant, and in the kind of love being a son or a servant calls for. It is between the freeing love of God and the possessive love of man.

And if any of us should feel that we are wise and those we care for merely children, let us remember that God is far more wise in relation to us than we can ever be to a child.

In my work with children's homes, and as I see both schools and families both inside and outside this work, this is the real, the basic difference between the good and the bad. It is not a difference in how much they have, or even how much they love (for love is a quality, not a quantity). It is not whether they are strict or lenient or believe in this or that rule or code of behavior but whether they respect children, not only as future adults, but for themselves here and now. Do they listen to them or are they always telling them things; do they love them in a way that frees them to fight their own

* Given to the Parent-Teacher Association, Kenwood Elementary School, Kendall, Florida, January 1961.

battles and to experience life to the fullest? Do they try to protect them from life, or try to make them into something that parent or teacher wants them to be? Some parents, teachers or houseparents insist that children must be grateful, or want to feel superior to children. Some take pleasure in studying children so as to feel wise and powerful themselves. Some treat children as objects to be used, or manipulated, but others treat them as subjects, as those whose feelings and actions are supremely important in themselves, and these are those who love a little as our Father loves each of us. And so I ask you to join with me in this prayer:

Oh, God, whose children we are, help us to model our parenthood or teacherhood more nearly on Thy love for us, that we may learn to treat our children with the respect accorded to us, as subjects of supreme importance and never as objects for our use. And this we ask in the Name of Him Who was Himself a human child, Who we know troubled His parents, but Whom they listened to and allowed to grow in grace and fulfill the destiny He had chosen—even our Lord the Christ, Jesus, Son of God and Son of Man.